CW01347112

Enabling Eco-Cities

Dominique Hes • Judy Bush
Editors

Enabling Eco-Cities

Defining, Planning, and Creating a Thriving Future

palgrave
macmillan

Editors
Dominique Hes
Thrive Research Hub, Faculty of
Architecture, Building and Planning
University of Melbourne
Parkville, VIC, Australia

Judy Bush
Thrive Research Hub, Faculty of
Architecture, Building and Planning
University of Melbourne
Parkville, VIC, Australia

ISBN 978-981-10-7319-9   ISBN 978-981-10-7320-5   (eBook)
https://doi.org/10.1007/978-981-10-7320-5

Library of Congress Control Number: 2018931907

© The Editor(s) (if applicable) and The Author(s) 2018
This work is subject to copyright. All rights are solely and exclusively licensed by the Publisher, whether the whole or part of the material is concerned, specifically the rights of translation, reprinting, reuse of illustrations, recitation, broadcasting, reproduction on microfilms or in any other physical way, and transmission or information storage and retrieval, electronic adaptation, computer software, or by similar or dissimilar methodology now known or hereafter developed.
The use of general descriptive names, registered names, trademarks, service marks, etc. in this publication does not imply, even in the absence of a specific statement, that such names are exempt from the relevant protective laws and regulations and therefore free for general use.
The publisher, the authors and the editors are safe to assume that the advice and information in this book are believed to be true and accurate at the date of publication. Neither the publisher nor the authors or the editors give a warranty, express or implied, with respect to the material contained herein or for any errors or omissions that may have been made. The publisher remains neutral with regard to jurisdictional claims in published maps and institutional affiliations.

Cover pattern © Melisa Hasan

Printed on acid-free paper

This Palgrave Pivot imprint is published by Springer Nature
The registered company is Springer Nature Singapore Pte Ltd.
The registered company address is: 152 Beach Road, #21-01/04 Gateway East, Singapore 189721, Singapore

To those working towards a thriving future, and to our kids and grandkids, and their place within the wonder and awe of our amazing planet.

Foreword

We have entered the so-called urban age—a time when human prospect depends as never before on the sustainability of cities and larger human settlements. The concept of the Anthropocene, widely debated in the sciences, reminds us that the future of non-human existence—indeed, planetary well-being—will be decided by our increasingly urban species. Aside from rapid urbanisation, a set of great and inevitable transitions is underway—in climate systems, human settlement and movement, the integrity of the biota, and political organisation and expression, to name a few. Epochal change is inevitable and in motion. The challenge is to prevent the destructive, limiting changes from gaining the upper hand and to give precedence and strength to those forces and aspirations that seek to turn the crisis around and drive us towards a new age of natural—*human and non-human*—flourishing.

In this context, my colleagues Dominique Hes and Judy Bush have produced a valuable, insightful, and timely collection of essays based on their discussions at the recent (July 2017) Ecocity World Summit, which was hosted in Melbourne, a city that choruses globally about its liveability. Who can argue with the notion of liveability, a notion that speaks directly to the fundamental, everyday experience of human life? And yes, as necessary and obvious as the term is, it is also clearly an inadequate expression of what we must strive for in an urban age imperilled by ecological risk and social stress. Questions of social justice (liveability for who?), ecological integrity, and the future well-being (resilience) come to the fore when we commit to a more critical, searching mindset.

This critical, searching outlook informs the essays in this volume that capture the conversations and wisdom manifest in the Ecocity World Summit sessions. What makes these contributions especially exciting and constructive is that they reach beyond critique to consider prospects and pathways to the flourishing future that surely beckons, even in the teeth of epochal crisis. The eight authors in this volume, essay the many transitions that will need to be made at a variety of scales, from local to global, in quest for a healed and renewed world. In sympathy with the Summit and their own values, the accent is on the positive and the possible, not simply the fearsome testimony of risk and stress that our cities too often now betray. Note the language they use—thriving, renewing, innovation, creativity, participation, enabling—which expresses what we must hold to, the excitement and possibility that always emerges when one order is giving way to another.

Three cheers for the Thrive Hub at the University of Melbourne and its growing circle of partners, friends and readers. *Enabling Eco-cities* is another important and impressive milestone in the journey of this research community which, as this volume attests, dedicates itself to 'To those working towards a thriving future; and to our kids and grandkids, and their place within the wonder and awe of our amazing planet'.

Director, Melbourne Sustainable Society Institute,   Brendan Gleeson
Melbourne, VIC, Australia
Co-chair Ecocity World Summit 2017

Preface

In 2017, the Ecocity summit series came to Melbourne, Australia. This global event, the latest in an impressive lineage of conferences held every two years since 1990, aimed to explore pathways to more sustainable, resilient, and equitable cities. Its six major themes, climate and energy transformations, food and water security, smart cities for people, healthy and caring cities, culturally vibrant cities, and governance, infrastructure and finance, defined the context in which questions of understanding, imagining and creating ecocities were posed.

The Ecocity summit provided the opportunity and impetus for organising a conference session that brought together the research of a diverse group of people, all past or present PhD students of mine, all researching the transitions towards more resilient, adaptive and sustainable cities. Our group includes a planner, an ecologist, an architect and a theatre designer, linked together through the work of the Thrive Research Hub of the Faculty of Architecture, Building and Planning of the University of Melbourne. Our research seeks to understand how cities can be thriving parts of a resilient future.

Our conference session asked, 'What is an ecocity? Is it the solution for the future and how can it be implemented?' Based on our research, we addressed these questions through the lenses of regenerative development and sustainability transitions. To contextualise this work Lars Coenen joined me to write on regenerative development, transitions and smart specialisation to operationalise it in the city. Tanja Beer and collaborators described ways to engage, connect, celebrate and innovate; Judy Bush used green space policy approaches to discuss policy success factors and narratives; Andréanne Doyon focused on understanding niches and how they support innovation and transition, and Angelica Rojas-Gracia presented case studies from three continents to show how design processes can achieve benefit and positive contribution.

Motivated by the active and enthusiastic response to our conference session, this book was created to disseminate our research and the practical tools and guidance to a wider audience. I hope that this book contributes towards practical efforts to create a thriving future in which our roles in environmental custodianship of the biosphere are underpinned by creativity, innovation, enthusiasm, a willingness to experiment and a sense of connection to people, place and culture at both local and global scales.

Parkville, VIC, Australia Dominique Hes
September 2017

Acknowledgements

Tanja Beer and colleagues extend heartfelt thanks to all the fabulous people and organisations involved in the Ephemera project, and to the Armidale community for their love and support.

Judy Bush's research was supported by an Australian Government Research Training Program Scholarship (previously Australian Postgraduate Awards) and a Low Carbon Living Cooperative Research Centre scholarship.

Andréanne Doyon's research was supported by a Melbourne International Research Scholarship.

Angelica Rojas-Gracia's research was supported by an Australian Postgraduate Awards and the Norman Macgeorge Scholarship.

Contents

1 Introduction: Creating Eco-Cities—From Sustaining to Thriving 1
Dominique Hes and Judy Bush

2 Regenerative Development and Transitions Thinking 9
Dominique Hes and Lars Coenen

3 Innovation: Creativity as a Renewable Resource for the Eco-City 21
Tanja Beer, David Curtis, and Julie Collins

4 Urban Green Space in the Transition to the Eco-City: Policies, Multifunctionality and Narrative 43
Judy Bush and Dominique Hes

5 Niches: Small-Scale Interventions or Radical Innovations to Build Up Internal Momentum 65
Andréanne Doyon

6 Benefit Driven Design Process: An Inclusive and Transdisciplinary Approach Towards Enabling More Resilient and Thriving Outcomes 89
Angelica Rojas-Gracia

7 The Problem, the Potential, the Future: Creating a Thriving Future 109
Dominique Hes and Judy Bush

Index 123

List of Contributors

Tanja Beer is an award-winning ecoscenographer (ecological stage designer) and an academic fellow in performance design and sustainability at the University of Melbourne, Australia. She has more than 20 years of professional experience, including creating designs for projects in Australia and oversees. Her practice-led research integrates public art and theatre-making with urban ecology. Tanja's most significant work is The Living Stage, an award-winning global initiative that combines stage design, horticulture and community engagement to create recyclable, biodegradable, biodiverse and edible performance spaces. Her work has also been featured in exhibitions at the V&A Museum (London) and the 2015 Prague Quadrennial.

Judy Bush is a researcher and lecturer in environmental policy and practice at the University of Melbourne. She recently completed her PhD, 'Cooling cities with green space: policy perspectives'. She has previously worked as the executive officer of the Northern Alliance for Greenhouse Action, a local government alliance in Melbourne working on climate change action, and at Merri Creek Management Committee, working on habitat restoration and community engagement. She has a Masters of Environmental Studies and a Bachelor of Science (Hons).

Lars Coenen is an interdisciplinary scholar cross-cutting the fields of innovation studies, economic geography and science and technology studies. His research interests converge around the geography of innovation: Why is it that some regions and cities in the world stand out in their ability to foster and diffuse novelty? What explains this spatial concentration of innovation in an era of globalization? How can regions and cities improve their capacity to innovate? In particular he is interested in addressing this broad set of questions on innovations related to pressing societal challenges such as climate change.

Julie Collins has a PhD in the ecological humanities (Charles Sturt University) and is an academic at the University of New England (UNE), working in the areas of indigenous studies, theatre studies and education. Julie is also a community artist and in 2016, was a co-creator of the eco-drama performed on Tanja Beer's Living Stage as part of the Black Gully Music Festival. Her research interests include the role of immersive theatre and storytelling in evoking empathy and transforming behaviour in environmental and social justice contexts. Julie is also currently researching the role of experiential learning on Country in Aboriginal education.

David Curtis is founder of EcoArts Australis Inc. An ecologist and social scientist, David holds an honorary position at the Institute of Rural Futures at the University of New England. His career has spanned ecological and sociological research, environmental restoration, education and outreach, and natural resource management policy. He has written extensively on rural and urban ecological sustainability and the arts and environmental behaviour. He organised several multi-arts events celebrating ecological sustainability, some of which have had audiences of thousands of people and participation of hundreds. He recently published a graphic novel about reversing eucalyptus dieback called *Dazed by Dieback*.

Andréanne Doyon is a lecturer in sustainability and urban planning at RMIT University. She completed her PhD at the University of Melbourne in the Faculty of Architecture, Building and Planning. Her doctoral thesis investigated how planning for urban resilience is informed by niche interventions. Currently, her research and teaching are focused on urban planning and governance related to sustainability and resilience. Previously, she worked for the City of Vancouver and the University of British Columbia in planning and research in sustainable development, urban revitalization and integrated thinking. She has a bachelor of arts and a master of arts planning from the University of British Columbia.

Dominique Hes is an award-winning author and educator in the field of sustainability and the built environment. Her work aims to constructively critique the current approach to development and to undertake grounded projects to investigate alternatives to current business and usual. This has led to the investigation of approaches such as regenerative development, positive development, biophilia, biomimicry and permaculture as models for future practice. With degrees in science engineering and architecture, she brings a multidisciplinary approach to understanding the current problems of attaining sustainability and future solutions to a thriving future.

Angelica Rojas-Gracia is an architect and PhD candidate at the University of Melbourne. Her research investigates the role that the design process can have in supporting the social-ecological system. She is co-founder of incluDesign, a collaborative practice that aims to support ecosystems while expanding the accessibility of design services to wider populations. She holds a position as senior urbanist at Ethos Urban and has taught design studios and regenerating sustainability subjects at the University of Melbourne. Angelica combines research and practice and is particularly interested in the feedback loops and synergies between practice, research and teaching.

List of Figures

Fig. 2.1	Cheonggyecheon river in Seoul, South Korea, before 'daylighting'. Source: CA Landscape Design Co., Ltd	13
Fig. 2.2	Cheonggyecheon river in Seoul, South Korea, after 'daylighting'. Source: CA Landscape Design Co., Ltd	13
Fig. 2.3	Zollverein, UNESCO World Heritage Site and the regional museum of the Ruhr Area. Source © Jochen Tack/Stiftung Zollverein	17
Fig. 3.1	Willow-weaving workshop with Steiner school students. Photo: Laszlo Szabo	28
Fig. 3.2	Building the Bower Stage with the Backtrack Boys. Photo: Laszlo Szabo	29
Fig. 3.3	Inside the Bower design with living globes created by the community. Photo: Laszlo Szabo	30
Fig. 3.4	The water scene from Armidale's ecodrama. Photo: Laszlo Szabo	32
Fig. 3.5	Storytelling for young children and their families in the Bower. Photo: Laszlo Szabo	33
Fig. 4.1	Policy domains that address urban green space	51
Fig. 4.2	Policy mechanism categories and the transition trajectory to eco-cities	55
Fig. 5.1	The s-curve (adapted from Rotmans et al. 2001)	71
Fig. 5.2	Multi-level perspective as a nested hierarchy (adapted from Geels 2002)	72
Fig. 5.3	Illustrations of change (adapted from Gunderson and Holling 2002)	77
Fig. 5.4	Planning for eco-cities through niche interventions	78

Fig. 6.1 Visual representation of the new school. Source: incluDesign   102
Fig. 6.2 Visual representation showing the children of village in their future school. Source: incluDesign   103
Fig. 6.3 Children of the village looking for representations of themselves in their future school. Source: FONA   104
Fig. 6.4 Cultural ceremony and performance celebrating a new beginning. Source: FONA   105

List of Tables

Table 4.1	Policy analysis framework, adapting Transition Management elements	48
Table 4.2	Urban ecosystem services and associated policy domains	50
Table 4.3	Urban green space policy mechanisms	53
Table 4.4	Policy mechanisms and associated outcomes sought	55
Table 4.5	Policy success factors	59
Table 6.1	Benefit-driven design process: Enabling capabilities and activities	101

CHAPTER 1

Introduction: Creating Eco-Cities—From Sustaining to Thriving

Dominique Hes and Judy Bush

Abstract How can eco-cities underpin urban thriving? Starting from the legacy of urban development to date, the chapter critiques current approaches to urban sustainable development. It reviews various definitions of eco-cities and outlines how these could contribute to a shift to ideas of thriving and abundance. Cities are places of potential with the bulk of humanity and its wealth within their boundaries. Cities need to develop in ways that harness this potential, through understanding how innovation, creativity, policy, planning and practice can create irresistible narratives of the future. Capturing people's hearts and minds will be key to transitioning to a more ecologically responsible and socially just future. This chapter introduces each of the book's chapters and how they contribute to the ability to achieve this shift.

Keywords Eco-city • Urban sustainable development • Thriving

D. Hes (✉) • J. Bush
Thrive Research Hub, Faculty of Architecture, Building and Planning, The University of Melbourne, Parkville, VIC, Australia

© The Author(s) 2018
D. Hes, J. Bush (eds.), *Enabling Eco-Cities*,
https://doi.org/10.1007/978-981-10-7320-5_1

An eco-city is an ecological city in balance with nature, living within its environmental means, a human habitat built with relationship to living natural systems. The concept of eco-cities, first proposed by Richard Register in his 1987 book, imagines cities as living systems, ecologically healthy and enhancing the health and well-being of both their human and non-human urban dwellers. It acknowledges the legacy of the destructive power of urban construction, yet also the creative potential in building and living in cities that seek to connect with the ecosystems in which they are located, and that contribute towards ecological restoration (Register 1987, 2006). Creating eco-cities brings together planners, environmental scientists, architects, urban designers and engineers (Tang and Wei 2010); 'the idea of an eco-city implies an agenda for society, culture, economics, and government with a vision and intention for action that stretches indefinitely into the future' (Downton 2017).

The strategies to achieve eco-cities include minimising energy, water and waste, such as through the use of renewable energy and reduced car use. They strive towards social, environmental and economic sustainability (Wong and Yuen 2011). But eco-cities and their designers and inhabitants need to go much further than a focus on sociotechnical efficiency. An eco-city seeks to connect with human imagination, creativity and ingenuity to create cities that are not just more efficient but that actually generate positive benefits. This calls for cities that 'actually build soils, cultivate biodiversity, restore lands and waters and make a net gain for the ecological health of the planet' (Register 2006, 1), that go beyond approaches that seek to be 'less bad' by minimising negative impacts and actually create positive benefits and positive impacts.

As eco-city ideas and concepts have developed and matured, so too have approaches to sustainability. Is it enough to understand sustainability as eco-efficiency, or as reducing the negative impacts of overuse of resources and energy? Where sustainability has been critiqued as an approach that focuses on efficiency, on measurement and on goals and targets, going beyond these approaches to envision 'thriving' eco-cities involves an expanded focus on well-being, on relationships and on fostering communities through an enhanced sense of affinity with each other and with the biosphere. Where sustainability includes a focus on optimisation, regenerative development and thriving creates space for experimentation and abundance that underpins the 'redundancy' or spare capacity required for resilience.

This book argues that what is holding us back from a thriving future is that we are trying to create sustainable outcomes that improve social and ecological well-being, within the same worldview or framework that created the degradation. After decades of working towards sustainability, findings from international studies, such as the Millennium Assessment Reports (MEA 2005) and the 2014 IPCC assessment report on climate change, indicate that the situation is getting worse, not better, prompting the Worldwatch Institute, in its 2013 State of the World report, to ask whether sustainability is still possible (Worldwatch Institute 2013). Our current framework structuring sustainability practice is couched in the language of quantitative, performance-based indicators reporting on performance in isolated categories, compliance with which is largely driven by individual interest: reputational, financial or simply avoiding prosecution. Much has been written about the flaws in this framework and its foundation in a 'mechanistic' worldview, as well as the need to shift towards a more relational worldview that will help us develop frameworks suitable for working with living systems (Hes and du Plessis 2015; Murray 2011).

1.1 The Need for a New Approach, a New Worldview

This more relational worldview is called by many the ecological worldview, and its needs highlighted in built environment practice as early as the 1960s by Ian McHarg (McHarg 1969). Since then numerous authors have explored the characteristics of the emerging ecological worldview and its main narratives (Goldsmith 1988; Capra 1997; Elgin and LeDrew 1997). The consensus is that the ecological worldview represents a shift from looking at the behaviour, performance and interests of individual 'parts' to considering the well-being of the whole as expressed through interdependent relationships—a web of life of which humans are irreducibly part. That is to design solutions that work at the biophysical level, within inherently nested systems, across scales including and most importantly at the mental level. The critical aspect here is the interrelatedness and connectedness of the world; in many respects, the current approach to sustainable development has forgotten to engage with the hearts and minds of people. It has forgotten that what we need to create is an irresistible narrative that will change behaviour not just because we have to but because we want to. Unfortunately the current irresistible narrative is based on the values of the mechanistic worldview, those of competition, imperialism and rationalism, a narrative that rewards power, monetary wealth and status. To transition to eco-cities requires a shift from striving for 'eco-efficient' sustainability (within what has been framed 'a mechanistic worldview'), towards thriving and regenerative development within an ecological worldview.

If the vision for the eco-city is limited to being a 'sustainable' city, then we have set the goal too low. We can do better than minimising our footprint, we can create a positive one; we can do better than zero carbon by aiming for positive; we can do better than protecting biodiversity, we can create greater diversity. We live on a finite planet, but energy and ideas are not finite, and our cities can provide the substrate to add capacity. For example, all the additional surface area in cities provides opportunities for increasing green space, energy and water collection and so on. Lastly we need to shift our language from problem-solving to potential, created through celebration and building on what already works.

A thriving future envisions eco-cities in which connections and synergies, understandings of cities as urban systems of stocks and flows (Birkeland and Schooneveldt 2003) and relationships create the abundance that underpins our flourishing (Hes and du Plessis 2015). A thriving future brings together the twin objectives of living within our environmental means on a finite planet and of creating abundance through working regeneratively in partnership with nature.

Creating an eco-city is not just about the ability to envision and create new cities of the future. We cannot start from scratch. Existing cities and their legacies of built form, urban infrastructures and social practices are the foundations for creating eco-cities. Cities are expressions of human ingenuity and the power of technological and engineering solutions. They contain the evidence of human development as well as of environmental degradation, loss of habitat, biodiversity collapse, climate change and pollution. To create the eco-cities of the future, we need to work within existing cities and understand the history of a place, the story of each city, its biophysical context and its economic, governance and social context, its people, cultures and practices.

Such understandings bring to life the social-ecological systems which form the basis for cities. Such understandings also underpin the necessary processes of engagement, communication, debate and negotiation inherent in processes of change and in shifts from old approaches to thriving futures. Furthermore developing deep understandings of the history of the city and its story of place is essential to enable reconnections with nature and the biosphere (Andersson et al. 2014; Elmqvist et al. 2013), to enable an eco-city's inhabitants to live within its environmental means.

Central to this is design, solving problems and creating potential through the creative synthesis that takes the parts and creates a greater whole. It is design based on principles of stakeholder engagement, a key stakeholder being nature, and the question: How can we best add value, create benefit and contribute to all stakeholders and systems? Cities hold the greatest potential for creating the benefit as they are a concentration of people, resources, money, innovation and diversity.

This book contends that the city is a place of potential: as such cities need to develop in ways that harnesses this potential. In this book, we explore how this could be achieved. We focus on how innovation, creativity, policy, planning and practice can create an irresistible narrative of the future. We argue that capturing the hearts and minds of stakeholders in the city will be key to being able to transition to a more ecologically responsible and socially just future. This will involve creating coherent narratives that bring together competing demands and that seek to find ways to create abundance, to meet needs within environmental means, rather than splintered narratives that necessitate trade-offs and compromise.

This book is focused on bringing together the findings of researchers from varied disciplines, including innovation studies, architecture, design, planning and governance. These researchers are using regenerative development and transition theories in their work to envisage how eco-cities could be planned, designed and created. The researchers share a focus on investigating the processes that underpin transitions to the cities of the future—eco-cities—yet bring their distinct disciplinary perspectives to elaborate and explore different aspects and elements of urban social-ecological systems and the processes of urban change and sustainability transitions.

Following this introductory chapter, Chap. 2 explores the conceptual framework that informs this book's analysis. It describes regenerative development and sustainability transitions, and shows how understanding the essence of place, its stocks, flows and relationships can support reconnection with nature, and initiate restoration of a city's ecological health and biodiversity. The chapter proposes that linking the entrepreneurial approaches of smart specialisation with the social-ecological perspectives of regenerative development can underpin the transition to eco-cities. Following this, Chaps. 3, 4, 5, and 6 consider how concepts of regenerative development and sustainability transitions can be applied to the creation of eco-cities, through the lenses of innovation, policy, niches and design. The chapters reinforce a focus on working across scales, both spatial and temporal, and linking culture, built form, ecology and governance.

Chapter 3 uses the case study of a theatre-making project to demonstrate how participatory design can create connections and empower communities across natural, constructed, economic and cultural systems, thereby contributing to the public's knowledge and care of their local environment. It argues that community arts has the potential to open up new ways of communication and new narratives that can respond to climate change and other environmental challenges. Through 'ecoscenography' (ecological stage design), the co-creation of the Bower Stage points towards the potential for connecting with intrinsic environmental values, and empowering and inspiring the participants towards care for environment and for each other.

Chapter 4 focuses on the green spaces in cities, and the public policies that seek to retain and maximise these urban spaces. It argues that urban green spaces, essential elements for eco-cities, provide multiple functions and benefits, from contributions to biophysical processes such as regulating urban heat and storm water, to aesthetics and recreation opportunities, and habitat for biodiversity. However, this multifunctionality presents challenges to the predominantly monofunctional governance systems in which urban policies operate. The chapter argues that communication and engagement play important roles in effective policy approaches. Shifting from the splintered narratives of green space's individual functions towards coherent narratives that encompass multifunctionality contributes to policy success.

Chapter 5 focuses specifically on how change unfolds in urban systems. It brings together the fields of urban planning, resilience studies and sustainability transitions. After reviewing, comparing and combining the literature from these three fields, it applies the findings to study the trajectory of small-scale 'niche' interventions, demonstrating how developing understandings of change processes in urban systems can illuminate the transitions to eco-cities.

Chapter 6 provides an architectural design perspective to creating eco-cities. It presents the 'Benefit-Driven Design Process', a set of enabling activities that can underpin participatory processes for design of new buildings and facilities. It seeks to go beyond a focus on physical infrastructure and instead aims to encompass and incorporate into the design process the significant yet intangible properties of place and community, contained within stories and practices and artefacts. In doing so, it reinforces the importance of understanding cities as social-ecological systems, and of committing time, as well as resources to building a shared vision and co-created design.

The book concludes by summarising the key lessons and tools presented in each of the chapters and demonstrating their application to address urban environmental challenges. In keeping with the book's focus on harnessing creativity towards solutions to environmental challenges, Chap. 7 reflects on how the approaches discussed in previous chapters can be applied to address the scenario of restoration of an urban waterway. The scenario serves as a microcosm or glimpse of the possibilities for a thriving future contained within transitions towards thriving eco-cities.

References

Andersson, E., S. Barthel, S. Borgström, J. Colding, T. Elmqvist, C. Folke, and A. Gren. 2014. Reconnecting Cities to the Biosphere: Stewardship of Green Infrastructure and Urban Ecosystem Services. *Ambio* 43 (4): 445–453. https://doi.org/10.1007/s13280-014-0506-y.

Birkeland, Janis, and John Schooneveldt. 2003. *Mapping Regional Metabolism: A Decision-Support Tool for Natural Resource Management*. Canberra: Land and Water Australia.

Capra, Fritjof. 1997. *The Web of Life: A New Scientific Understanding of Living Systems*. London: Flamingo.

Downton, Paul. 2017. Seven Things you Need to Know About Ecocities. *The Nature of Cities*. https://www.thenatureofcities.com/2017/03/05/seven-things-need-know-ecocities/. Accessed November 9, 2017.

Elgin, Duane, and Coleen LeDrew. 1997. *Global Consciousness Change: Indicators of an Emerging Paradigm*. San Anselmo, CA: Millennium Project.

Elmqvist, Thomas, Michail Fragkias, Julie Goodness, Burak Güneralp, Peter J. Marcotullio, Robert I. McDonald, Susan Parnell, Maria Schewenius, Marte Sendstad, Karen C. Seto, Cathy Wilkinson, Marina Alberti, Carl Folke, Niki Frantzeskaki, Dagmar Haase, Madhusudan Katti, Harini Nagendra, Jari Niemelä, Steward T.A. Pickett, Charles L. Redman, and Keith Tidball. 2013. Stewardship of the Biosphere in the Urban Era. In *Urbanization, Biodiversity and Ecosystem Services: Challenges and Opportunities. A Global Assessment*, ed. Thomas Elmqvist, Michail Fragkias, Julie Goodness, Burak Güneralp, Peter J. Marcotullio, Robert I. McDonald, Susan Parnell, Maria Schewenius, Marte Sendstad, Karen C. Seto, and Cathy Wilkinson, 719–746. Dordrecht: Springer.

Goldsmith, E. 1988. Rethinking Man and Nature: Towards an Ecological Worldview. *Ecologist* 18 (4–5): 118–185.

Hes, Dominique, and Chrisna du Plessis. 2015. *Designing for Hope: Pathways to Regenerative Sustainability*. Abingdon: Routledge.

McHarg, Ian. 1969. *Design with Nature*. New York: Natural History Press.
MEA. 2005. Environmental Degradation and Human Well-Being: Report of the Millennium Ecosystem Assessment. *Population and Development Review* 31 (2): 389–398.
Murray, Paul. 2011. *The Sustainable Self: A Personal Approach to Sustainability Education*. London: Earthscan.
Register, Richard. 1987. *Ecocity Berkeley. Building Cities for a Healthy Future*. Berkeley, CA: North Atlantic Books.
———. 2006. *Ecocities: Rebuilding Cities in Balance with Nature*. Rev. ed. Gabriola, BC: New Society Publishers.
Tang, Zhenghong, and Ting Wei. 2010. Introduction. In *Eco-city and Green Community: The Evolution of Planning Theory and Practice*, ed. Zhenghong Tang. New York: Nova Science Publishers.
Wong, Tai-Chee, and Belinda Yuen. 2011. Understanding the Origins and Evolution of the Eco-City Development: An Introduction. In *Eco-City Planning: Policies, Practice and Design*, ed. Tai-Chee Wong and Belinda Yuen, 1–14. Dordrecht: Springer.
Worldwatch Institute. 2013. *State of the World 2013. Is Sustainability Still Possible?* Washington: Island Press.

CHAPTER 2

Regenerative Development and Transitions Thinking

Dominique Hes and Lars Coenen

Abstract Regenerative development is a whole systems approach that partners people and their places, working to make both people and nature stronger, more vibrant and more resilient. It aims to increase the vitality, viability and adaptability of a place through understanding its story, its flows and how developing positive relationships enhance the potential of all stakeholders. Key to working regeneratively in an eco-city is understanding the essence of place and what needs to be strengthened to enable adaptation through future change. Smart specialisation is a process through which understandings of the socio-technical potential of the system can seed entrepreneurial opportunities and new positive relationships. When this is broadened to the social-ecological perspective underpinned by regenerative development, it can guide our transition to a thriving eco-city.

Keywords Regenerative development • Smart specialisation • Innovation

---

D. Hes (✉)
Thrive Research Hub, Faculty of Architecture, Building and Planning,
The University of Melbourne, Parkville, VIC, Australia

L. Coenen
Melbourne Sustainable Society Institute, The University of Melbourne,
Parkville, VIC, Australia

2.1 Introduction

Regenerative development is a whole systems approach that partners people and their places, working to make both people and nature stronger, more vibrant and more resilient. It aims to increase the vitality, viability and adaptability of a place through understanding its story, its flows and looking at developing positive relationships by always looking to enhance the potential of all stakeholders. Key to working regeneratively in an eco-city is to understand the essence of place, what is critical to that city and needs to be strengthened to be able to adapt through future change. Understanding change by analysing sustainability transitions processes can further support adaptation and provide guidance and strategies for future change processes. Smart specialisation, with its focus on experimentalism, stakeholder analysis and entrepreneurial discovery has the potential, when partnered with regenerative development, to guide and operationalise transitions to thriving eco-cities. This chapter provides an overview of regenerative development and sustainability transitions, and demonstrates how smart specialisation can support their operationalisation. The chapter concludes by outlining ten steps to understanding the potential of place.

2.2 Understanding Regenerative Development and Sustainability Transitions

To understand the essence of place at the city level is to think of the city as a complex ecosystem, unique to its specific geology, hydrology, climate and other biophysical flows. Yet, this would be looking at a city without its people. Therefore it is also critical to look at its flows related to its history, its industries, the way it is seen by other cities and the rest the world, its governance, its education, its economy, its policies and so forth. This allows you to understand the city and its social and ecological context but still does not allow you to work regeneratively or ecologically in its transition towards a more sustainable and resilient place.

> Essence can be defined as the true nature or distinctive character that makes something what it is; the permanent versus the accidental element of being. (Mang et al. 2016, 48)

If we look ecologically on how a system adapts to change, this happens through the ability of niches to create points of innovation that allows the reallocation of resources as a system goes through change. These niches then expand and influence the system. A forest does not appear overnight nor does it restore after a fire overnight, it takes time building on what works, what has survived and what is thriving to restore to its new normal. Yet again, this is working on the biophysical level. If we now bring people into this conversation, we can see the key potential we bring is our ability to learn from the past and project to the future, our intuition, our ability to experiment and adapt consciously and constructively. We can start seeing the potential of regenerative development—bringing the ecological and the human together in mutual reciprocity through social agency.

In the context of transition to an eco-city, towards a more social-ecologically resilient thriving place, it is therefore important to use this concept of niches as places of experimentation and innovation together with people's potential to dream forward and actively design the experiments. Further, this needs to occur in the context of the essence of the city to inform the design of the experiments within the niche. To do this, the regenerative development approach would argue, there needs to be a strong understanding of that niche's or place's identity, purpose, role and ability to influence the city and contribute to the expression of its essence. This is what *Regenesis* would say is that place's unique 'story' (Mang et al. 2016).

In determining the story of a niche, it is important to understand the flows that move through it and bring it to life. These flows should include the social-ecological, the socio-technical and the contextual. Examples of the social-ecological are the biophysical elements of air, light, materials, water, animals (both human and non-human), plants and soil. Examples of the socio-technical are infrastructure, technology, industry, government and education. And the contextual are history, community, culture and religion. Flows do not necessarily neatly fit into these three arbitrary categorisations, but are useful in thinking about the different components that go into making a city, or urban ecosystem, thrive.

Yet though these flows may be moving through the place, it is not until we look at their relationship to that place that the potential for innovation and experimentation becomes apparent. It is in the relationship of air, light, materials, water and infrastructure, technology and history, community and culture that the opportunities contributing to these flows through creating positive relationships emerge. A famous example to illustrate this is the Cheonggyecheon stream in Seoul, South Korea.

> The stream was first called Gaecheon ('open stream') and was part of an ongoing method of drainage out of the village that is now called Seoul from the Joseon Dynasty (1392–1897) onwards. It was renamed to Cheonggyecheon when Japan occupied the country between 1910 and 1945. The stream began to be covered over in 1958 after the Korean War due to the increased rural to urban migration, resulting in deterioration of the condition of the stream. This took over 20 years and culminated in the construction of an elevated highway over it in 1976. At that point, this was seen as the height of industrialisation and modernisation. Yet in 2003 then Mayor Lee Myung-bak proposed to remove the highway and restore the stream so as to reintroduce nature to the city, to promote a more environmentally friendly green presentation of the area and to restore some of the history and culture. Restoring the stream was not as easy as just daylighting, as its neglect had resulted in it almost drying up; today it requires ongoing pumping of water from other areas such as the Han River, its tributaries and groundwater from subway stations.
>
> Yet now the stream has a renewed relationship with the site. This has resulted in a reduction of the urban heat island (Philipp et al. 2015), the return of birds, fish and insects, it is a place for festivals or just having a lunch, it encourages walking and it has increased property value and commerce in the area. Further the reduction of car traffic through downstream transport planning increase in buses and subway use has resulted in improved air quality. It is therefore not the stock of the water that is as important as how it is brought into relationship with the site and its contribution to the story of 'who' this place is (Figs. 2.1 and 2.2).

Flows are critical in understanding what brings a place to life, and it is at the heart of understanding the story of that place. An analogy here could be how a person becomes who they are in the world: it is a combination of how the flows of their past (education, culture, family, opportunities, etc.) and how they see themselves now (mother, CEO, teacher, nurse) allows them to be in the world.

Fig. 2.1 Cheonggyecheon river in Seoul, South Korea, before 'daylighting'.
Source: CA Landscape Design Co., Ltd

Fig. 2.2 Cheonggyecheon river in Seoul, South Korea, after 'daylighting'.
Source: CA Landscape Design Co., Ltd

An example of the power of this story is Melbourne, 'the world's most liveable city', or Silicon Valley's story of being the centre of all IT innovation. Once a place has found a story that resonates with its people, then decisions and investments are made to reinforce this story, it drives its development. If we look to how ecosystems develop we can see that they do so slowly, innovation often starting within niches, bringing together flows into relationships that previously did not occur. In human systems this can be planned for: that is once the flows are understood, initiatives can be introduced to test whether mutually beneficial relationships can be created between these flows. Using the above ecological model, this is done in a niche and if successful allows the niche to shift towards becoming a more resilient and adaptive system.

In the Cheonggyecheon river example, the whole system has become more resilient because the urban heat island has been reduced, people are spending more time outside, air quality is improved and so forth. Yet this Korean example is not regenerative. Regenerative development is not only about building the capacity of the external systems ecology, economy and so on to be stronger; it is also about building the internal systems and capacity. This is the key to regenerative development: how do we work to optimise performance, create vibrant viable systems externally and do the same internally. In the Seoul example, you can ask the question: how are the people of this area of Seoul facilitated to continually grow adapt and build their capacity and potential in relationship with this place?

How then do we translate this notion of regenerative development into a viable strategy for urban renewal and development that creates or adapts an eco-city? What governance model can conceive of the whole systems approach that regenerative development embodies? Clearly, top-down development and planning models would be incompatible with the non-linear, evolutionary and emergent dynamics of regenerative development. On the other hand, bottom-up, grassroots modes of governance may lack breadth and sensitivity for the complexity to oversee the whole systems approach in a comprehensive way.

Regenerative development stipulates a number of guiding principles for the design and governance of eco-city change strategies. These principles are place-based, transformative, participatory and experimental. Firstly, regenerative development for eco-cities does not follow a universal blueprint but acknowledges the diversity of urban form and systems and should therefore be deeply anchored in and aligned with the uniqueness of place. Secondly, even though it departs from existing flows in a city, regenerative development does not seek to optimise the system(s) but rather to transform it and be future-facing. Thirdly, it requires citizen and stakeholder engagement in decision-making: this is needed not only to make sure that a strategy taps into the often tacit and socially distributed knowledge about the essence of place but also to secure legitimacy for change and reduce liabilities of newness. Fourthly, a strategy needs to acknowledge the inherent risks and uncertainties involved in regenerative development. There are no off-the-shelf, quick fixes available but strategies need to embrace innovative sometimes unproven and unorthodox solutions.

2.3 Smart Specialisation: Operationalising Regenerative Development and Sustainability Transitions

Learning from the limitations of one-size-fits-all blueprints for regional and urban development, current approaches pioneered in Europe under the paradigm of Smart Specialisation emphasise strategy development that adheres to these principles albeit in a more narrow context of regional economic development. The concept of Smart Specialisation signals a new phase in the evolution of urban and regional policy in Europe, based on more than two decades of experience with multi-level governance across a wide variety of territorial contexts in Europe. Smart Specialisation builds upon existing capabilities, resources and assets in a region as well as inclusive participatory governance arrangements to identify opportunities for development (Foray 2015).

According to the European Union S3 Platform, it is a place-based approach characterised by the identification of strategic areas for intervention based both on the analysis of the strengths and potential of the economy and on an Entrepreneurial Discovery Process (EDP) with wide stakeholder involvement. It is outward-looking and embraces a broad view of innovation including but certainly not limited to technology-driven approaches, supported by effective monitoring mechanisms.

To explain the approach, it can be broken down into three constitutive parts:

- Smart: S3 builds on an ex-ante analysis of the assets and resources available to regions and on their specific economic, social and environmental challenges in order to identify unique opportunities for development.

- Specialisation: S3 is focused on unique strengths supported by a critical mass of activity and capabilities across the region that supports technological as well as practice-based and social innovation.
- Strategy: S3 identifies a limited set of priorities for development where to concentrate investment. This should not be a top-down, picking-the-winner process but an inclusive EDP in which the quadruple helix of private sector, the research and education sector, civil society and government are discovering and producing information about new activities, jointly assesses the outcomes and empower those actors most capable of realising this potential. This includes a sound monitoring and evaluation system as well as a revision mechanism for updating the strategic choices.

It is precisely this EDP that distinguishes the smart specialisation approach and that sets it apart from previous paradigms in urban and regional development policies. Through the EDP the conceptualisation of innovation is more than 'taking a technology to the market' as it involves linking knowledge and its societal use. Rather than a straightforward discovery, it is better understood as a trial-and-error experimentation process in which existing knowledge is used and combined, new knowledge is created, suitable routines are elaborated upon, opportunities for societal use are screened and combinations of knowledge, routines and societal use are tested and continually adapted.

Taking this notion of innovation and experimentation into the context of regenerative development, it points to the importance of social learning through networks of distributed actors that jointly develop, transfer and apply knowledge, change behaviour and adapt institutions to protect, nurture and mainstream novelty in niches. This often involves institutional entrepreneurship as actors break with existing rules and practices associated with the dominant logics and institutionalise the alternative rules, practices or logics they are championing.

Having a research and innovation strategy for smart specialisation has become an ex-ante conditionality for regions to receive investments from the European Regional Development Fund. Consequently there are over 120 strategies designed and developed at the regional level within the EU. However, to provide an illustrative example of this approach, we need to resort to a more historical case where a strategy not only has been conceived but also implemented and evaluated. The 'revitalisation' of the German Ruhr Valley serves as a good example of regenerative development that draws heavily on key principles of smart specialisation 'avant la lettre' (even before the term 'smart specialisation' emerged).

2.3.1 The Ruhr Valley

The Ruhr Valley of northwestern Germany has been a centre for coal (and steel) production in Europe since the middle 1800s. Since the 1970s however, the region has witnessed industrial decline and rising unemployment. By the 1990s, about two-thirds of the coal, steel and related industry jobs were gone. Today, the Ruhr has become one of the key centres for environmental industry, technology and research in Germany. Local firms, universities, research institutes (e.g. the Soil Protection Centre and the Environmental and Packaging R&D Centre) and environmental agencies cooperate closely. Also, former mines and steel factories are currently used for tourist purposes ('industrial culture'): having been one of Europe's largest industrial coal complexes, Zollverein is now a UNESCO World Heritage Site and a dynamic cultural place with a variety of museums for industrial history and design, like the red dot museum and the Ruhr Museum (Fig. 2.3). Zollverein is also a business location and serves as a centre for many cultural events. Guided tours in different languages on the 'Monument Path' (Denkmalpfad) offer insights into the once largest coal mine in Europe.

Fig. 2.3 Zollverein, UNESCO World Heritage Site and the regional museum of the Ruhr Area. Source © Jochen Tack/Stiftung Zollverein

The State government has been central to the process of shaping these regeneration strategies, acting in partnership with municipalities, universities and private actors. The way the neo-industrialisation approach towards structural change was organised departed from the ways and approaches of the past. The late 1980s and 1990s witnessed the beginning of new bottom-up development approaches, guided by regional planning and key State (Land) institutions but designed and implemented by local groups. The renewal from within approach was organised in close dialogue with and met with approval in the local community. The Emscher River International Building Exhibition (IBA) heralded this new approach.

From the early 1900s, the Emscher River had become a wastewater open sewer for local industry and households. It was considered the country's most polluted river and in the 1980s characterised by vacant factories, closed mines and abandoned docks, sinking ground from mining and large heaps of mining residues and dams. The approach of the Emscher IBA—with the official subtitle 'Workshop for the Future of Old Industrial Regions' was innovative and new. Established by the Ministry of Urban Development, Housing and Transport for the State of Northrine-Westphalia, its aim was to be an answer to the complex economic, social and ecological problems of the Emscher subregion and, secondly, an attempt to give an internationally recognised example of state-led economic, social and ecological restructuring of old industrial areas. The initiative lasted from 1989 to 1999 and invited proposals from all sectors of society, be it municipalities, companies, pressure groups or individuals, to address five themes for restructuring the area: the renovation of the Emscher landscape into parkland, ecological regeneration of the Emscher River system, development of new work locations in derelict industrial sites, development of new housing forms and urban district and new uses for industrial buildings and industrial monuments.

The approach used to implement the IBA initiative has served as a vehicle for institutional entrepreneurship for renewal with processes and procedures of regional policy and governance. In 10 years 123 cooperative projects were implemented, varying from the setting up of technology centres to the renovation of apartments and the restoration of industrial monuments for tourist purposes. It is however this very role of providing a local and inclusive participation framework combined with top-down quality control as an alternative to previously more centralised policy and governance approaches that constitutes the success of the IBA initiative in restructuring the Ruhr. First and foremost, the IBA provided an organisational form for dialogue and collaboration between stakeholders that led to the inception of 'regional development coalitions', that is, bottom-up, horizontally based co-operation between different actors in a local or regional setting based on a socially broad mobilisation and participation of human agency. The establishment of such regional development coalitions has been an important foundation for the build-up of new industries in the Ruhr based on processes of community participation and engagement.

2.4 Take-Home Tool and Approach: 10 Steps to Understanding the Potential of a Place

1. Create a core team of people who participate in the process from development of the understanding of place to the identification and implementation of the priorities.
2. Map aspects of the place such as hydrological, geomorphological and ecological.
3. Map the stocks and flows that bring a place to life—its history, natural flows, climate, money and so on.
4. Using these flows look through major events over the place's history and look at the flows that had an impact—positive and negative.
5. Using this understanding look at the relationships between the flows and the place that created these impacts.
6. Identify key patterns of this place and develop a sense of the role this place plays in the larger system—this will help identify its story.
7. Use 'Smart: S3' to identify unique opportunities for development based on the positive relationships mapped above.
8. Use 'Specialisation: S3' to focus on the unique patterns and strengths of the place by initiating a critical mass of activity and capabilities that builds on the identified positive relationships.
9. Use 'Strategy: S3' to identify a limited set of priorities for development where to concentrate investment. These priorities should be co-created with the people of the place.
10. Integrate a feedback and reflection process both for the development of the viability, viability and ability to thrive of the place as well as those involved in the project.

REFERENCES

Foray, Dominique. 2015. *Smart Specialisation: Opportunities and Challenges for Regional Innovation Policy.* Abingdon, Oxon: Routledge.

Mang, Pamela, Ben Haggard, and Regenesis. 2016. *Regenerative Development and Design: A Framework for Evolving Sustainability.* Hoboken, NJ: Wiley.

Philipp, Conrad Heinz, Joullanar Wannous, and Parisa Pakzad. 2015. *Thermal Impact of Blue Infrastructure: Casestudy Cheonggyecheon, Seoul (Korea).* ICUC9-9th International Conference on Urban Climate jointly with 12th Symposium on the Urban Environment, France, 20–24 July 2015.

CHAPTER 3

Innovation: Creativity as a Renewable Resource for the Eco-City

Tanja Beer, David Curtis, and Julie Collins

Abstract Cities need new strategies for conservation and climate change resilience that engage global narrators, unite diverse perspectives and mobilise an increasingly despondent public. This chapter examines community arts as a potential resource for the eco-city, including how incorporating creative perspectives into sustainability communication can open up new ways of thinking about how cities are reimagined for an ecological paradigm. Community arts can provide a unique platform for empowering communities across natural, constructed, economic and cultural systems, thereby contributing to the public's knowledge and care of their local environment. Using a participatory design and theatre-making project as a case study (The Bower Stage, Armidale, Australia, 2016), the chapter demonstrates how incorporating both creative and ecological perspectives can enrich environmental citizenship and connection for the eco-city.

T. Beer (✉)
Thrive Research Hub, Faculty of Architecture, Building and Planning, The University of Melbourne, Parkville, VIC, Australia

D. Curtis
Institute of Rural Futures, University of New England, Armidale, NSW, Australia

J. Collins
School of Humanities, University of New England, Armidale, NSW, Australia

© The Author(s) 2018
D. Hes, J. Bush (eds.), *Enabling Eco-Cities*,
https://doi.org/10.1007/978-981-10-7320-5_3

Keywords Ecoscenography • Eco-theatre • Community arts
• Participatory design • Ecodrama • Place-making

3.1 Introduction

To create a thriving future, leading sustainability experts contend that cities need to incorporate place-based, community-orientated and transdisciplinary systems that enable positive contribution to social and ecological function and evolution of the city (Bennett and Beudel 2014). Nevertheless, current models that dominate our cities are built upon the mechanistic structures that favour reductionist and siloed thinking, making transdisciplinarity and more inclusive practices difficult to pursue.

A number of commentators (e.g. Schumacher 1973; Rees 1995; Capra 1996; Hawken et al. 1999; Hofstra and Huisingh 2014; Collins in press) have drawn attention to this dominant anthropocentric worldview, which since the end of the eighteenth century has encouraged us to see ourselves as separate from nature—to view the world as something to be analysed and exploited with little regard for environmental consequences. Ecofeminist philosopher and historian Carolyn Merchant (1980) explains how it is largely this separated thinking and reductionist view of the world that has propagated a disconnection from nature, leaving us unbalanced in our understanding of ecology and the living world. This perspective has also dominated discourses of sustainability, largely distancing and disconnecting us from the problems at hand, while limiting the efficacy of our engagement with the living world (Bateson 1972; Clayton and Radcliffe 1996). It has also placed limits on creativity, favouring instead mechanistic modes of production that can lead to quantitative, measureable or calculate-able outcomes. While mechanistic viewpoints have been incredibly valuable for furthering sustainability, their focus on limitation and mitigation tend to lack more holistic and inspired actions (Hes and du Plessis 2015).

This chapter focuses on the potential for creativity and community-based arts practice to be a resource for the eco-city. The arts are consistently undervalued as a means for engaging meaningfully in sustainability discourse. Sustainability discussions are dominated by environmental scientists, sociologists and economists and tend to overlook the role of the arts in ecologically sustainable development. It is common to read books on sustainability and environmental policy which make no mention of the arts (e.g. Bierbaum 1991; Toyne 1994; Beder 1996; Goldie et al. 2005; Low et al. 2005; Coffey and Marston 2013). Environmental organisations and agencies tend to see the arts, at best, as a means of communicating a message and therefore marginal to the real concerns of environmental action (Curtis 2007).

Nevertheless, researchers are increasingly stressing the importance of the arts in communicating ecological concepts in ways that encourage connection, resilience, empathy and care (Bingham 2012; Curtis 2003, 2006, 2009, 2010, 2011, 2017; Curtis et al. 2013; Curtis et al. 2014; Kagan and Kirchberg 2008). Artists can be masters of uniting conflicting or siloed viewpoints and presenting ideas in a way that is non-confrontational and nondidactic as well as being fun, engaging and inspiring. Put simply, they can offer a much needed and unique perspective to other disciplines within the sustainability sector, particularly when approaching the concept of the eco-city.

Recent research suggests that a cognitive understanding of scientific concepts does not necessarily facilitate tangible and constructive action on global issues (Evans 2014). As María Heras and J. David Tàbara (2016, 949) argue, 'boosting imaginative competences, enthusiasm, and hope, and not simply imposing rational thinking with the usual dumping of gloomy facts, is of paramount importance to trigger collective learning and transformative action'. Transdisciplinary and creative practice has been identified as an essential component of tackling the complex problems of the future for regenerative development (Hadorn 2008). For example, a recent project at the University of New South Wales, *Curating Cities*, looked at the potential contribution of public art to sustainable urban development (Bennett and Beudel 2014). This research advocated for artists to be included at the conception stage of development—to be present at 'the beginning of a system'– rather than as adornment, promoting the creative capacity of the arts to generate ideas and solutions to the environmental problems (Bennett and Beudel 2014, 8).

Incorporating creative perspectives into sustainability communication and discourse opens up exciting new avenues for exploration—including new ways of thinking about how cities and regional centres are reimagined for an ecological paradigm. This chapter examines the potential of artists as community advocates whose unique skills as lateral thinkers, communicators and provocateurs can bring new perspectives into reimagining urban spaces. We discuss ways in which creative practitioners can provide a platform for empowering communities across natural, constructed, economic and cultural systems, thereby contributing to the public's knowledge and care of their local environment.

Using an ecological arts project (The Bower Stage, Armidale, NSW, 2016) as a case study, we explore how participatory design and collaborative storytelling can play a valuable role in facilitating ecological understanding and empathy to enrich environmental citizenship and connection.

3.2 Collective Storytelling, Immersive Theatre and Participatory Design as Connecting Devices for the Eco-City

David Eisenberg and Bill Reed (2003) describe collaborative storytelling as a valuable tool for sustainable development. Actively and respectfully empowering and catalysing communities entails adopting new narratives, perspectives, parameters and skills (Fuad-Luke 2009, 147–148). Sharing experiences and aspirations can be 'an emotional mortar' where participants engage in creative practices and 'layers of meaning' that activate personal, aesthetic and ecological sensibilities (Fuad-Luke 2009, 100–101). As Dominique Hes and Chrisna du Plessis (2015, 201) contend, it is by placing people's own stories within the larger socio-ecological narrative that allows communities to 'weave together' and open up 'previously unimagined possibilities'. In particular, multisensory and live storytelling platforms (such as theatre and performance) have the potential to enhance learning through bodily and experiential knowledge (Sullivan et al. 2015; Stevenson 2014).

Stories can play an important role in communicating complexities, helping to collectively deepen connections and reimagine futures, and acting as powerful agents of change, permeating psychosocial spheres and influencing the lives of those connected to them (Mang and Reed 2012, 29–30). A growing body of literature indicates the importance of engaging people on a visceral, emotional and creative level in order to activate behaviour change (Thomsen 2015). Multisensory knowledge, such as touch, smell and movement, are also important to understanding our environment and the laying down of memory (Pye 2016). Indeed, neuroscientists have discovered that compelling narratives change the chemistry of our brain and have the power to affect our attitudes, beliefs and behaviours (Zak 2015). As eco-playwright Teresa J May (2013, 193) writes, 'stories create a matrix of belonging, a living tissue between past and present, and between human and non-human communities; and in this way, stories help heal the earth and ourselves'. It is through embracing social-ecological narratives that we can begin to heal our relationship with the more-than-human world (du Plessis 2012, 19).

Creating transformational experiences through narrative and performance can be enhanced by techniques of 'immersive theatre', which allows audiences to experience a narrative and spatial design more intimately. In immersive theatre, audience members are not passive bystanders. They are part of the story; their role may be as a witness or even an additional character. This contrasts with more conventional modes of theatre production, where audiences sit silently in the dark watching actors on a well-lit stage, feeling comforted, or defeated by the outcome. Augusto Boal (2000), who created a Theatre of the Oppressed, saw theatre as a tool for creating social change, empowering audience members through facilitating their participation and interaction in the performance. Immersive theatre invites the audience to share the same space with performers—where experiences may include touch, taste, smell and movement (Alston 2013, 331). The power of immersive theatre is therefore enhanced by the multi-sensual experience it provides, which can increase people's understanding and memory of stories.

In conjunction with theatre making, other 'immersive activities'—such as community gardening, collaborative design and crafting—can play a meaningful role in creating collective identities across sustainability initiatives. Hands-on activities can be an opportunity to form collective identities, increase socio-ecological awareness and connectivity (Beer and Hernandez 2017). In their recent book, *Through Vegetal Being* (2016), philosophers Luce Irigaray and Michael Marder also argue that it is also through 'vegetal' (or plant relating) activities in particular (e.g. touching and smelling plants) that our relations with the more-than-human world can be reignited. One way that humans can connect with nature is through co-creative activities with living plants and natural materials. Marder and Irigaray refer to these kinds of creative tasks as one that activates 'vegetal being', a mode of meaningful engagement with the natural world that reveres its presence and agentic capacities. These ideas are also integral to ecoscenography (ecological stage design), a concept that brings performance design into an increased awareness of broader ecologies and global issues: to conceptualise ways in which an ecological ethic can be incorporated into theatre and stage design practices (Beer 2015, 2016a, b).

In this paper, we use ideas of collective storytelling, immersive theatre and participatory design as a way of bringing communities together, to not only voice their concerns and hopes for the future but also to partake in constructing built environments that integrate socio-ecological potential. We explore how the eco-theatre and ecoscenography can make an integral contribution to discourses around environmental issues—including how immersive performance spaces can invoke emotional responses such as empathy, to act as stimuli for change.

3.3 Introduction to the Black Gully Festival and *Ephemera* Project

In order to demonstrate the value of hands-on creativity and participatory storytelling in advocating for the eco-city, we examine a recent project, The Bower Stage as part of *Ephemera*, curated by EcoArts Australis Inc. (founded by Curtis) and supported by Festivals Australia in 2016. The Black Gully Festival is an annual event (since 2010) that takes place as part of the Environment Science Community Arts People Entertainment programme, in the regional city of Armidale, NSW, Australia. The event was initiated to celebrate the active ecological restoration of the Black Gully site by the Armidale community adjacent to the New England Regional Art Museum (NERAM). Every year, it includes a diversity of performances by local musicians, as well as an array of stalls from local artisans and sustainability groups.

In 2016, EcoArts Australis Inc. worked with the Black Gully Festival to create *Ephemera*, a project which invited a group of ecological artists to create works that embraced the concept of ephemerality in response to the restoration site (EcoArts Australis 2017). The Bower Stage was one of the curated works initiated by Beer (ecological stage designer and community artist) with performances staged by students from Armidale High School and Duval High School (in collaboration with Collins). Beer worked with emerging artists, community members and theatre practitioners in the months leading up to the festival to design and construct The Bower Stage for the Black Gully Festival. Four other artists were employed to create ephemeral artworks for the festival. These included an eel trap sculpture woven from *Lomandra longifolia* using traditional Aboriginal weaving practices by two Indigenous weavers Amy Hammond (Gomeroi artist and weaver) and Gabi Briggs (Anaiwan artist and weaver); intimate ephemeral artworks created from natural materials along the creek by Greer Taylor (ephemeral artist and poet); and unfired pottery made from the clay dug from the Black Gully creek and impregnated with native plant seeds by Andrew Parker (local ceramic artist and community cultural development practitioner).

Our research into *The Bower Stage* was examined through a mixed methods research methodology (Tashakkori and Teddlie 1998) where the majority of the inquiry was developed through the implementation of the work and its practice-led reflection-in-action. Data was collected via field notes, journal notation and photographs. In this chapter, we reflect on our own experiences of the project and how these insights can inspire the future of the eco-city.

3.4 Building The Bower Stage

The concept of The Bower Stage originated out of Beer's Living Stage project—a global ecoscenography initiative which combines stage design, horticulture, botanical crafting and community engagement to create recyclable, biodegradable, biodiverse and edible performance spaces. Armidale's Living Stage (entitled The Bower Stage) was central to the celebration of the newly restored Black Gully, behind NERAM, which has increasingly become a hub for environmental and creative activity. The project was created by Beer in collaboration with Melbourne designer Ashlee Hughes and local artist Simon Mellor.

The aim of The Bower Stage was to create a platform for sharing stories through gardening, food, music and performance—bringing people together to strengthen community bonds. Inspired by artists such as Nicholas Henry, John Dougherty and Andy Goldsworthy, our idea was to create a bower—a cosy, magical and shared space that could house multiple communal storytelling performances amongst an existing circle of pine trees on the site adjacent to the creek. The exchange of community and ideas was central to the making of The Bower. Community members from all walks of life contributed to its creation, including people of all ages and abilities.

As the design was intended to contribute to the Black Gully Festival and the regeneration of the creek, locally found and natural materials were chosen to facilitate the design. Hughes and Mellor guided community members in collecting branches, logs, sticks and leaves for the construction of the dome-like space. Willow and other non-native plants (weeds that were impacting the local ecology of the creek) were cut to create the walls and roof structure of The Bower in collaboration with the local Steiner school while a local disability arts group took part in decorating the space (Fig. 3.1). Two Indigenous teenagers from Armidale's Backtrack Boys (a programme which helps youth 'get back on track' by getting involved in community projects) were also invited to take part (Fig. 3.2).

Fig. 3.1 Willow-weaving workshop with Steiner school students. Photo: Laszlo Szabo

Fig. 3.2 Building the Bower Stage with the Backtrack Boys. Photo: Laszlo Szabo

The boys chopped branches, adding foliage to the design, making seats from tree stumps and contributing ideas to the space. Their endless energy resulted in a beautiful 'bower' space, which the boys described as their 'secret hiding spot' to come back to.

The design also included finding household objects from the local tip shop to hold edible plants which were grown in collaboration with the nearby local community garden. Mellor was especially instrumental in sourcing materials for the creation of the stage—regularly calling upon his friends and neighbours to assist with finding natural and reclaimed materials when necessary, and thereby connecting local knowledge with design processes. These found artefacts contributed to the quirky and creative flavour of the design—reclaimed window frames were hung between the trees, bottomless chairs from the tip shop were filled with edible plants from the local community garden, while an empty bird cage (donated by a community member) was suspended from one of the branches.

In order to celebrate and contribute to the biodiversity of the site, we also worked with the Armidale Tree Group to create native living plant sculptures that could be featured as part of the Black Gully Festival celebrations. These would then be replanted into the creek bed after the festi-

Fig. 3.3 Inside the Bower design with living globes created by the community. Photo: Laszlo Szabo

val. The plant sculptures were inspired by the Japanese art of 'kokedama' where a plant's root system is wrapped in moss and bound with string, transforming it into a sculptural and suspended art form. This exercise in 'vegetal crafting', through multiple free workshops leading up to and over the course of the festival, was a unique way of engaging families, teenagers, seniors and children of all abilities in the appreciation of natural beauty, where ideas of biodiversity, fragility, humility, adaptation and growth were moulded and wrapped into spherical forms. Each moss ball was lovingly crafted and hung in the space to create a suspended forest of living globes (Fig. 3.3).

Overall, the flexible and inclusive design process allowed the design to be inspired by local materials and people, allowing community stories to be woven into the process. The end result was an ecoscenographic design that was site specific and responsive and one that was extremely integrated with the local socio-ecological environment—a physical depiction of the many hands that shape a community.

3.5 Creating the Armidale Ecodrama

Using The Bower Stage as their inspiration and performance space, Collins (lecturer and theatre practitioner), Camille Dunsford (high school drama teacher) and Katy Walsh (high school drama teacher) created an ecological-themed theatre production (or 'ecodrama') which engaged students from three local high schools in devising theatre that explored environmental issues. The aim of the performance was to raise consciousness and inspire change, as well as examine idea's place, identity and community with young people of the local area. Ecodrama can be defined as theatre which allows us to deepen our awareness of 'ecological identities as people and communities' (May 2007). It explores the reciprocal connection between humans and the more-than-human world (Abrams 1997).

The Bower Stage's ecodrama was modelled on the style of vaudeville where the audience were invited to enter 'The Environment' (presented as a pristine and precious commodity) and journey up a pathway circled by the pine trees. The high school students were encouraged to research topics on the global ecological crisis, including climate change, water security, human impacts on the environment, and society's individual and collective responsibility for change (Collins et al. in press). Our aim was to encourage children to actively have a voice in regard to their future and to reflect on and express their own concerns and aspirations.

The immersive space of The Bower Stage aimed to enhance the sensual involvement and psychological engrossment of the audience (Machon 2013). Audience members were allowed into The Environment in small groups, supervised by a tour guide to absorb the earthy smell of the native vegetation amongst an array of peculiar characters and tableaux, such as a bearded moss lady who described the health and beauty benefits of moss, two characters in picture frames debating climate change, a scene where characters were fighting over buckets of clean water from the nearby Black Gully creek (Fig. 3.4), and an intimate tableaux of violinists playing for a tea party of plants, before inviting audiences to 'nibble' at home-grown lettuce and strawberries. As they left the performance space, spectators visited the Fortune Teller, who gave them a 'personal reading' on a tarot card with an environmental message (provided to each person as they entered the space), which focused on the individual responsibility to take environmental action.

The Bower Stage audience encompassed a very broad demographic, including many families and children who were excited at seeing their own

Fig. 3.4 The water scene from Armidale's ecodrama. Photo: Laszlo Szabo

community perform for them. The immersive and multi-sensual nature of the ecodrama resulted in many people reporting that they felt moved by the performance. This may have also been partly due to the environmental messages being delivered by children and young people—those who will be most impacted by humanity's inaction on environmental issues. By delivering an ecological story told by high school students for their local community, it was hoped that 'a seed of good intention' was planted in the hearts and minds of participants and audience alike (Collins, Beer and Dunsford in press).

Approximately 200 people (of all ages and abilities) participated in the making of The Bower Stage and ecodrama performances preceding the Black Gully Festival, with another 2000 people attending the festival. The organisers of the festival noted how the making of The Bower Stage and its performances helped actively engage a diversity of people in celebrating the ecological restoration of the site, as well as highlighting greater ecological concerns for the community. The audience at the festival included a broad range of participants from many cultural backgrounds, including adults and families with young children in attendance during the day for storytelling in The Bower (Fig. 3.5), and a preponderance of teenagers

Fig. 3.5 Storytelling for young children and their families in the Bower. Photo: Laszlo Szabo

later in the evening that used the Bower space as a chill-out room. The proximity of NERAM to the site was also useful in breaking down the stereotype of art being a space of 'white upper-middle-class privilege' and encouraging a broadening of the demographic that felt a sense of connection to the site.

3.6 Discussion

On the basis of our experiences, we found that avenues like the Black Gully Festival can provide a platform for showcasing sustainability with and for communities that can also become a framework for engaging in larger eco-city challenges in a way that is constructive, inclusive and creatively inspiring. Community participation in the creation of The Bower Stage and the corresponding ecodrama demonstrated many attributes of the eco-city, including the use of locally found resources, zero-waste design, contribution to the restoration of environmentally damaged urban areas, enabling opportunities for a range of community members (including more disadvantaged groups), supporting the local ecology, and increasing awareness of environmental and sustainability issues. Participatory arts events can be particularly valuable for changing attitudes and behaviours towards the environment, because of their capacity to generate meaningful social interactions between people. As community artist Rosi Lister explains:

> To make something with somebody else, you're observing, you're communicating, ideas are forming. As they form and you're communicating, things are growing and that all becomes a very rich social process, and the more that those social processes are being constructed and made through creativity, the more they become tangible. (Lister in Curtis 2007)

According to Lister, the reason that the participatory arts are valuable in changing environmental behaviour is the pleasure that people gain from the art-making process and the sense that they are simultaneously and collectively contributing to something bigger than themselves. The coming together to create something, 'to make something happen', is the very essence of community capacity-building for environmental sustainability. For while a community that has high social capital may not necessarily be ecologically sustainable, it is our proposition that a community that is ecologically sustainable will have high levels of social capital, because ecological sustainability requires coordinated collective action, rather than every person thinking only of themselves (dictatorships excepted). This sense of 'collectivity' was witnessed by designer Ashlee Hughes, who observed what might be described as the aspiring characteristics of an eco-city:

> Armidale seems to be a very creative community, people are involved in their local environment, the community garden is thriving and a hub of activity, the gallery is filled most days with workshops and locals swinging by … there is a strong local indigenous culture which was great to discover and learn more about … and is important when working on country … locals saw the progression of the design, children played in it as it was being made and added their own sticks and design ideas … I also got to know the community garden and spent many a day having a mint tea and biscuits amongst the flowers. Some art groups working at the gallery also helped us in the creation of kokedamas, which became spontaneous workshops for whoever was interested, allowing for interaction and impromptu community involvement … Working on the "bower stage" has been one of the most creatively rewarding projects I've ever worked on. The main aspect I would highlight is the sense of community that was felt, the moment I arrived in Armidale I

felt welcomed and a sense that I could ask any questions, talk to anyone, be curious and really become a part of the community for a short time. (Ashlee Hughes, email message to authors, December 6th, 2016)

As demonstrated by Hughes' experience, community arts practice can be valuable platform for connecting to local people and places, opening up opportunities for shared communication of ideas and values. We propose that The Bower Stage provides three key action points that could be applied to the Ecocity. These include:

1. Invite multiple creative, cultural perspectives and narratives into place-based actions.

Participatory art has the capacity to flow across boundaries, opening up new places for social interaction. It builds bridges between places and people, both physically and metaphorically, creating conversations of 'possibilities' rather than 'limitations'. As demonstrated through The Bower Stage, creating opportunities for different social, cultural and generational groups to come together can be a mortar for future collaboration and resilience in the face of global crisis. Co-creating performance spaces with communities can bring people together to exchange ideas and empower them to take action on larger issues. It can be a participatory civic act, able to make lasting impacts on the equity and involvement of a community, neighbourhood and city. Incorporating creative activities that emphasise the sharing of culture can stimulate empathy and critical thinking in the face of great adversity.

2. Allow children to have agency in the co-creation of their future through their artistic expression.

Preparing our future generations for uncertainty will not only involve guiding our children to be resilient and adaptable to change but also empowering them to directly experience what it means to care for their environment and become part of positive transformation (Somerville and Green 2015). This entails providing opportunities for young people to relate and contribute to their local ecosystems while strengthening their capacities to work with others as active citizens in building ecological resilience and social connection to create forward thinking actions. Projects like The Bower Stage can bring children into community discussions in a way that encourages them to use their creativity to express themselves and their ideas. Thus, having children as part of sustainability conversations can open up new perspectives for the creation of a thriving and inclusive city.

3. Embrace the potential of smaller creative projects to help bring people together to practice and celebrate ecological ways of thinking and being.

Small community arts projects have the capacity to bring people together to test out new ways of doing things that are capable of contributing 'positive, mutually reinforcing, enduring benefits to human and ecological systems' (Robinson and Cole 2015, 4). Participatory arts practices like The Bower Stage allow communities to openly celebrate creativity and collaboration. It's all about making sustainability fun, embracing people's creativity and dissolving perceptions of powerlessness by giving voice to everyday people and their stories. The acknowledgement and celebration of small achievements can also galvanise opportunities for larger initiatives, elevating the community's voices on sustainability issues in a positive and constructive way.

3.7 Conclusions and Avenues for Further Exploration

As highlighted in our introduction, the role of the arts in moving Australia towards environmental sustainability is often overlooked by policymakers, academics and planners. While the conceptualisation of the eco-city includes 'culture' as one of its four principles, its emphasis appears to be on encouraging social equity and diversity, rather than on the creative capacity of humans and the value of the arts for sustainable development. We suggest that this requires reframing in order to embrace the potential for the arts to shape environmental behaviour through aiding in the communication of sustainability and cultural vitality. As highlighted above, community arts can open up new public engagement tools and strategies that can examine ways in which creative practice can sow the seeds of ecosystem restoration and community vitalisation. Given this, we argue that we should not only be aspiring to become eco-cities but to also nurture processes that are simultaneously both ecological and creative.

The foregoing begs the following question: could a place become an eco-city without the incorporation of community arts? As demonstrated through The Bower Stage, the arts can provide a valuable and readily made platform for aiding communication across age groups and disciplines, creating empathy for socio-ecological systems. It can be an inspiring space for engaging communities in discussing ideas that have the potential to shape the economic, social, cultural and environmental attributes of the region. Without the injection of creativity and imagination, we run the risk of building cities that are devoid of beauty, diversity and pleasure—the very aspects that draw us to them in the first place.

Australia's environmental impact is driven by consumption that is high in embodied energy, water and resources. While the arts can be used in the promotion of materialism and consumption (as can be the case in more elitist artistic platforms), they can equally well be used in the promotion of sustainability. As demonstrated by our case study, participatory arts in particular can contribute to an ecologically sustainable society through their ability to foster a spirit of altruism rather than materialism (Cunningham 1994, 1996). Participatory arts events have a social-capital building role that can assist in communities fostering a celebration of environmentally sustainable behaviours and aspirations (e.g. Curtis 2006, 2009).

The question may now be posed as to how projects like The Bower Stage could contribute to larger aspirations of the eco-city? First of all, we suggest that creative projects can offer new ways to engage communities with 'stories of place' through constructive, performative, narrative and experiential site-based approaches. Considerations for collective narratives might include stories of how urban spaces have transformed past ecosystems, performances that demonstrate how multi-layered historic and contemporary landscapes intersect with human trajectories and spatial hierarchies, and how these stories might be revealed to audiences through new forms of communication. By incorporating creative engagement as a tool for environmental and social remediation, a project might blend cultural and scientific methodologies to ask: 'How can we engage audiences to reveal urban nature, and provoke humanity's intrinsic emotional connection with nature?'; 'How can creativity deliver ecological understanding of environmental adaption and resilience?'; and 'How can artistic practices reveal pathways for community involvement in environmental stewardship, and cultivate hope for the future?'. This presents exciting potentialities for further research.

Importantly, we posit that projects like The Bower Stage can provide an opportunity to think creatively and with imagination about environmental issues, outside the box of politics and pure instrumental value—they allow us to consider the intrinsic value of our environment and those things that cannot be explained purely by rationality. By promoting a cohesive social and environmental sustainability, an integrated concept of human and environmental well-being, the arts can inspire change in hearts and minds and empower and inspire people to take action. As Dave Carr, director of the Black Gully Festival, explains, 'care for environment and an artistic sense are both signs of a civilised society—when combined together they are a civilising influence' (Carr in Curtis 2007).

3.8 Take-Home Tool and Approach: Using Creativity for Sustainability in the Eco-City

1. Invite multiple creative, cultural perspectives and narratives into place-based actions.
2. Allow children to have agency in the co-creation of their future through their artistic expression.
3. Embrace the potential of smaller creative projects to help bring people together to practice and celebrate ecological ways of thinking and being.

References

Abram, David. 1997. *The Spell of the Sensuous: Perception and Language in a more-than Human World*. New York: Vintage Books.

Alston, Adam. 2013. Audience Participation and Neoliberal Value: Risk, Agency and Responsibility in Immersive Theatre. *Performance Research* 18 (2): 128–138.

Bateson, Gregory. 1972. *Steps to an Ecology of Mind*. New York: Ballantine Books.

Beder, Sharon. 1996. *The Nature of Sustainable Development*. Newham: Scribe Publications.

Beer, Tanja. 2015. The Living Stage: A Case Study in Ecoscenography. *Etudes* 1 (1): 1–16.

———. 2016a. Ecomaterialism in Scenography. *Theatre and Performance Design* 2 (1–2): 161–172.

———. 2016b. Reimagining the Ruins of Scenography. *ASAP/Journal (Association for the Study of the Arts of the Present)* 1 (3): 487–511.

Beer, Tanja, and Cristina Hernandez. 2017. Refugium WA: Crafting Connection Through Plant-Relating Arts-Science Experiences of Urban Ecology. *Nordic Journal of Science and Technology Studies* 5 (2): 30–43.
Bennett, Jill, and Saskia Beudel. 2014. *Curating Sydney: Imagining the City's Future*. Sydney: University of New South Wales Press.
Bierbaum, Nena. 1991. *Towards Ecological Sustainability*. Bedford Park: Flinders University: Flinders Press.
Bingham, Shawn Chandler, ed. 2012. *The Art of Social Critique: Painting Mirrors of Social Life*. Maryland: Lexington Books.
Boal, Auguste. 2000. *Theater of the Oppressed*. London: Pluto Press.
Capra, Fritjof. 1996. *The Web of Life: A New Scientific Understanding of Living Systems*. New York: Anchor Books.
Clayton, Anthony M.H., and Nicholas J. Radcliffe. 1996. *Sustainability: A Systems Approach*. Boulder: Westview Press.
Coffey, B., and G. Marston. 2013. How Neoliberalism and Ecological Modernization Shaped Environmental Policy in Australia. *Journal of Environmental Policy & Planning* 15 (2): 179–199.
Collins, Julie. in press. We All Stand on Sacred Ground: Promoting a Sustainable Land Ethic. Chapter 28. In *Building Sustainability with the Arts: Proceedings of the 2nd National EcoArts Australis Conference*, ed. David Curtis. Newcastle upon Tyne, UK: Cambridge Scholars Publishing.
Collins, Julie, Tanja Beer, and Camille Dunsford. in press. *Saving the Planet with Ecodrama: Transformational and Experiential Theatre within a Living Stage*. Proceedings Restore, Revegetate, Regenerate Conference, University of New England, February 2017.
Cunningham, Chris. 1994. *A Philosophical Framework for Urban Planning: The Concept of Altruisitic Surplus*. Paper presented at the P.A.P.E.R. Conference, University of New England, Armidale NSW, December 6.
———. 1996. A Philosophical Framework for Urban Planning: The Concept of Altruistic Surplus. In *Urban Habitat: The Environment of Tomorrow*, ed. G.G. Van der Meulen and P.A. Erlekins, 86–96. Eindhoven: Eindhoven University of Technology.
Curtis, David J. 2003. The Arts and Restoration: A Fertile Partnership? *Ecological Management and Restoration* 4 (3): 163–169.
———. 2006. Mobilising Rural Communities to Achieve Environmental Sustainability Using the Arts. *Agricultural Economics Review* 17 (1): 15–25.
———. 2007. *Creating Inspiration: How Visual and Performing Arts Shape Environmental Behaviour*. PhD Thesis, University of New England, p. 500.
———. 2009. Creating Inspiration: The Role of the Arts in Creating Empathy for Ecological Restoration. *Ecological Management and Restoration* 10 (3): 174–184.
———. 2010. *Plague and the Moonflower:* A Regional Community Celebrates the Environment. *Music and Arts in Action* 3 (1): 65–85.

———. 2011. Using the Arts to Raise Awareness, and Communicate Environmental Information in the Extension Context. *Journal of Agricultural Education and Extension* 17 (2): 181–194.

———., ed. 2017. *Building Sustainability with the Arts: Proceedings of the 2nd National EcoArts Australis Conference*. Newcastle upon Tyne: Cambridge Scholars Publishing.

Curtis, David J., Mark Howden, Fran Curtis, Ian McColm, Juliet Scrine, Thor Blomfield, Ian Reeve, and Tara Ryan. 2013. Drama and Environment: Joining Forces to Engage Children and Young People in Environmental Education. *Australian Journal of Environmental Education* 29 (2): 182–201.

Curtis, David J., Nick Reid, and Ian Reeve. 2014. Towards Ecological Sustainability: Observations on the Role of the Arts. *S.A.P.I.EN.S. Surveys and Perspectives Integrating Environment and Society* 7 (1): 15.

du Plessis, Chrisna. 2012. Towards a Regenerative Paradigm for the Built Environment. *Building Research & Information* 40 (1): 7–22.

EcoArts Australis. 2017. http://www.ecoartsaustralis.org.au/ephemera/. Accessed March 29, 2017.

Eisenberg, David, and Bill Reed. 2003. *Regenerative Design: Toward the Re-Integration of Human Systems within Nature*. Pittsburgh Papers: Presentations from the Greenbuild Conference.

Evans, Eleri. 2014. How Green Is my Valley? The Art of Getting People in Wales to Care About Climate Change. *Journal of Critical Realism* 13 (3): 304–325.

Fuad-Luke, Alastair. 2009. *Design Activism: Beautiful Strangeness for a Sustainable World*. London: Earthscan.

Goldie, Jenny, B. Douglas, and B. Furnass. 2005. *In Search of Sustainability*. Collingwood: CSIRO Publishing.

Hawken, Paul, Amory B. Lovins, and Hunter Lovins. 1999. *Natural Capitalism: Creating the Next Industrial Revolution*. Boston: Little, Brown and Co.

Heras, María, and David J. Tàbara. 2016. Conservation Theatre: Mirroring Experiences and Performing Stories in Community Management of Natural Resources. *Society & Natural Resources* 29 (8): 948–964.

Hes, Dominique, and Chrisna du Plessis. 2015. *Designing for Hope: Pathways to Regenerative Sustainability*. Hoboken: Taylor and Francis.

Hadorn, Gertrude Hirsch. 2008. *Handbook of Transdisciplinary Research*. London: Springer.

Hofstra, Nynke, and Donald Huisingh. 2014. Eco-Innovations Characterized: A Taxonomic Classification of Relationships Between Humans and Nature. *Journal of Cleaner Production* 66: 459–468.

Irigaray, Luce, and Michael Marder. 2016. *Through Vegetal Being: Two Philosophical Perspectives*. Columbia University Press.

Kagan, Sacha, and Volker Kirchberg, eds. 2008. *Sustainability: A New Frontier for the Arts and Cultures*. Waldkirchen: Verlag fur Akademische Schriften.

Low, Nicholas, Brendon Gleeson, Ray Green, and Darko Radovic. 2005. *The Green City: Sustainable Homes, Sustainable Suburbs*. Sydney: University of New South Wales Press.

Machon, Josephine. 2013. *Immersive Theatres: Intimacy and Immediacy in Contemporary Performance*. Basingstoke: Palgrave Macmillan.

Mang, Pamela, and Bill Reed. 2012. Designing from Place: A Regenerative Framework and Methodology. *Building Research & Information* 40 (1): 23–38.

May, Theresa J. 2007. What is Ecodrama? Earth Matters on Stage. http://pages.uoregon.edu/ecodrama/whatis/.

———. 2013. Indigenous Theatre in Global Times: Situated Knowledge and Ecological Communities in Salmon Is Everything and Burning Vision. In *Performance on Behalf of the Environment*, ed. Richard D. Besel and Jnan A. Blau, 193. Lanham, MD: Lexing-ton books.

Merchant, Carolyn. 1980. *The Death of Nature: Women, Ecology, and the Scientific Revolution*. San Francisco: Harper & Row.

Pye, Elizabeth, ed. 2016. *The Power of Touch: Handling Objects in Museum and Heritage Context*. Abingdon: Routledge.

Rees, William E. 1995. Achieving Sustainability: Reform or Transformation? *Journal of Planning Literature* 9 (4): 343.

Robinson, John, and Raymond J. Cole. 2015. Theoretical Underpinnings of Regenerative Sustainability. *Building Research & Information* 43 (2): 133–143.

Schumacher, Ernst Friedrich. 1973. *Small is Beautiful: A Study of Economics as if People Mattered*. London: Blond and Briggs.

Somerville, Margaret, and Monica Green. 2015. *Children, Place and Sustainability*. Basingstoke: Palgrave Macmillan.

Stevenson, Richard J. 2014. The Forgotten Sense: Using Olfaction in a Museum Context: A Neuroscience Approach. In *The Multisensory Museum: Cross-Disciplinary Perspectives on Touch, Sound, Smell, Memory, and Space*, ed. Ninna Levent and Alvaro Pascual-Leone, 151–166. Rowman & Littlefield.

Sullivan, Regina M., David A. Wilson, Nadine Ravel, and Anne-Marie Mouly. 2015. Olfactory Memory Networks: From Emotional Learning to Social Behaviors. *Frontiers in Behavioral Neuroscience* 9: 36.

Tashakkori, Abbas, and Charles Teddlie. 1998. *Mixed Methodology: Combining Qualitative and Quantitative Approaches*. Thousand Oaks: Sage.

Thomsen, Dana C. 2015. Seeing Is Questioning: Prompting Sustainability Discourses Through an Evocative Visual Agenda. *Ecology & Society* 20 (4): 242–250.

Toyne, Phillip. 1994. *The Reluctant Nation*. Sydney: ABC Books.

Zak, Paul J. 2015, January. Why Inspiring Stories Make us React: The Neuroscience of Narrative. Cerebrum: The Dana Forum on Brain Science 2015, Dana Foundation.

CHAPTER 4

Urban Green Space in the Transition to the Eco-City: Policies, Multifunctionality and Narrative

Judy Bush and Dominique Hes

Abstract Urban green space provides multiple benefits to city dwellers—both human and non-human. These 'nature-based solutions' include mitigating urban heat and stormwater runoff, providing biodiversity habitat and contributing to human health and wellbeing, and social and cultural processes, which are key elements in creating ecological cities. In the transition to eco-cities, public policies for urban green space provision can make substantial contributions. However, in the transition from existing mono-functional, mechanistic policy approaches, there are challenges in creating a vision for urban green space that navigates beyond the splintered narratives of single-function priorities. This chapter investigates how urban green space policies in Melbourne, Australia address these challenges, and the roles that communication, engagement and narrative play.

Keywords Urban green space • Nature-based solutions • Sustainability transitions • Urban policies

J. Bush (✉) • D. Hes
Thrive Research Hub, Faculty of Architecture, Building and Planning,
The University of Melbourne, Parkville, VIC, Australia

4.1 Introduction

As cities strive to address environmental, social and economic challenges and transform towards eco-cities, policies for urban green space must be part of this transition. Eco-cities are 'ecological cities in balance with nature' (Register 2006); urban green spaces are vital in eco-cities because they are the key locations for a wide range of ecological functions and processes. Furthermore urban green spaces provide the opportunities for people to have contact and connection with nature within cities. The aim of this chapter is to investigate how urban green space policies can contribute to the transition to eco-cities. In particular, we ask how policies can contribute to retaining and maximising urban green space.

Green spaces are essential elements for urban sustainability and thriving. Urban green spaces provide multiple benefits and ecosystem services to both the human and non-human city dweller. City planners have long recognised the recreation and aesthetic values of including green space in cities. More recently, green spaces' contributions to management of stormwater quality and quantity, as well as mitigation of heat and air pollution, have been recognised. In addition, there is a growing awareness of the role of green space for biodiversity, and for urban dwellers' opportunities for contact with nature, to promote physical and mental wellbeing, as well as providing opportunities for social and community wellbeing, and broader development of stewardship of the biosphere. Understandings of the city, and of urban contexts, are being reframed to include ideas of biodiversity and threatened species conservation, as well as food production and urban agriculture.

These multiple functions are key elements in the transition to eco-cities, using 'nature-based solutions' to address both local and global-scale challenges. As cities continue to develop, change and grow denser and broader, the inclusion of green space throughout urban areas is a necessary element for the creation of eco-cities, and the roles of public policy in retaining and maximising green space are brought into focus.

However, in the transition from our existing mono functional, mechanistic approaches to infrastructure provision, our governance systems are not equipped for the multifunctional nature-based systems that overlap or bridge between policy domains and departmental boundaries. Furthermore, within the multiple benefits, functions and forms of green space, there are challenges in creating a coherent and unified vision for this diversity, which is able to navigate beyond the existing splintered narratives and the competing priorities that promote the importance of one form or function over another.

This chapter first provides an overview of the functions, benefits and framings of urban green space within research and practice. Following this we present the results of our research on the green space policies for Melbourne, Australia. We discuss our findings on policies' mechanisms and key policy success factors. We reflect on the role of policy narrative and vision in either addressing or exacerbating the challenges of multifunctional green space within mono functional governance approaches.

4.2 Background

Green spaces have been part of human settlements and cities from earliest times, with gardens found in the stories, myths, legends and archaeological records of urban areas, the Hanging Gardens of Babylon, being one of the most famous urban gardens of antiquity (Turner 2005). Gardens and green spaces have been valued for their aesthetics and for the recreation opportunities they provide. They have also been seen as a refuge from the dirt and pollution of cramped city streets. As urban planning approaches developed at the start of the twentieth century, green spaces' recreation and aesthetic values were highlighted, particularly in planning approaches such as the Garden City movement in Britain (Fainstein and DeFilippis 2016). Likewise, and arguably strongly influenced by British approaches, Melbourne's first metropolitan strategy (MTPC 1929) also identified the importance of inclusion of green spaces within the city for recreation and aesthetic purposes.

Conceptualisations of the roles of urban green space have expanded, informed by more sophisticated and holistic understandings that incorporate the science of urban ecology (McPhearson et al. 2016b) and urban environmental sustainability (Grimm et al. 2008). Urban ecology developed from studies of ecology *in* cities, which focused on urban biodiversity, to ecology *of* cities, with a broader focus on urban ecological processes and functions (Douglas and James 2015). At the same time, conceptualisations of cities and urban systems are shifting from understanding them as socio-technical systems, to encompassing social-ecological systems (Wolfram and Frantzeskaki 2016; McPhearson et al. 2016a; Elmqvist et al. 2013). There has also been a growing understanding of the links between access to green space and human physical and mental health and wellbeing (Trundle and McEvoy 2016).

The ecosystem services concept sought to reflect the multiple benefits, both biophysical and cultural, within a framework that categorised the roles into supporting, provisioning, regulating and cultural services typology

(MEA 2003). Within this typology, a subset of these services are particularly important in urban areas, including climate and temperature regulation and stormwater management (regulating services), as well as the cultural services of placemaking for community and social interactions and educational, spiritual and aesthetic contributions and opportunities for active or passive recreation (Gómez-Baggethun et al. 2013). Birkeland (2008) highlighted the role the built environment can play in generating healthy ecological conditions through the provision of 'eco-services'. Urban green spaces are clearly significant locations for provision of many of these urban ecosystem services. The ecosystem services framework has been widely utilised in both environmental and social sciences research. However, aside from a few instances (e.g. CoM 2012), the 'ecosystem services' term has not diffused outside research to be widely utilised in policies and practice, particularly in Australia.

'Green infrastructure' terminology expands approaches to green space beyond provision of individual parks and gardens, to landscape-scale planning for an integrated, multifunctional and connected network (Benedict and McMahon 2006). While the term seeks to speak the language of urban planners, engineers and managers, by framing green space as part of urban infrastructure, it is understood and applied in different ways. It lacks consistent definition across research and practice communities, being applied in different ways by different people. These include quite specific applications, such as built installations of plants for specific engineering functions, to more general conceptions of urban green space that encompass the principles of multifunctional and connected green space, to any type of environmental sustainability-focused installations, including solar photovoltaic panels or bicycle lanes (Mell 2012; Bosomworth et al. 2013; Trundle and McEvoy 2016). In addition, it can be argued that the use of the term 'infrastructure' reinforces the focus on the 'regulating' services and functions of green space in urban processes: stormwater management and mitigation of heat and air pollution. These three functions have become the dominant urban ecosystem services identified in both research and practice. By doing so, other urban ecosystem services, particularly the cultural services, may be rendered less visible.

'Nature-based solutions' is a recently proposed term to encompass the simultaneous provision of human wellbeing and biodiversity benefits (Cohen-Shacham et al. 2016; EC 2015). This term seeks to provide an umbrella concept for ecosystem-related approaches that include ecosystem conservation and restoration, issue-specific approaches including climate change adaptation and mitigation, and infrastructure provision. The term is yet to achieve widespread use in Australian research or policy, though it has potential for creating a more strongly shared and consistent definition to underpin the integration of urban greening, for its multiple services and solutions, into the built environment (Xing et al. 2017). This chapter uses the term 'urban green space' (intentionally general and broad) to encompass the range of vegetated spaces throughout the city, from street trees and water-sensitive urban design and other green infrastructure treatments to parks, gardens, playing fields and waterways.

While there is a growing understanding of the multiple services, functions and solutions provided by green space, conceptualisations of urban green space as multifunctional green infrastructure or nature-based solutions are not yet widespread amongst urban planners and managers in Australia. As such, this research frames green space policy approaches, within the context of growing understandings of ecosystems services and nature-based solutions, as being in the early stages of sustainability transitions towards eco-cities. Theories of sustainability transitions seek to understand and investigate processes of change as part of long-term system transformations. Within the 'multilevel perspective' of sustainability transition theories (Geels 2002), green space policies could be understood as being still essentially 'niche' policies within the 'regime' of the broader urban policy suite. The multilevel perspective has developed understandings of the transition pathways along which niches may coalesce and challenge regime approaches (Geels and Schot 2007). The governance aspects and elements of sustainability transitions have been explored within Transition Management research (Rotmans et al. 2001; Loorbach 2010, Frantzeskaki et al. 2012, Frantzeskaki et al. 2014), defining four key areas of governance activity to support transitions: strategic, tactical, operational and reflexive. These four elements form the basis for this research's analysis of green space policies in Melbourne, and their application will be elaborated further in the following sections.

4.3 Methods

To investigate the role of policies in retaining and maximising urban green spaces, we analysed green space policies for Melbourne, Australia. Melbourne is located in south-east Australia. It is Australia's second most populous city and spans more than 10,000 km². There are three levels of government in Australia: federal, state and local. Melbourne is the capital city of the state of Victoria, with 32 local governments covering the metropolitan area. We take a qualitative research approach to investigate policies from the three levels of government.

We used the urban ecosystems services framework to first identify the policy domains across the three levels of government within which green space may potentially be addressed. Based on the identification of relevant policy domains, we then identified the key high-level policies for each domain from federal, state and local governments. We reviewed the content of these policies to determine if green space provision is addressed within these policies. Using this preliminary review we then analysed the key policies across three policy domains that were found to be most significant in addressing green space provision: *land use and cities, urban green space* and *climate change adaptation*. To focus the analysis on how policies can contribute to retaining and maximising urban green space in the transitions to eco-cities, we applied a policy analysis framework that utilises Transition Management's *strategic, tactical, operational* and *reflexive* categories, each with associated elements (Table 4.1). We supplemented analysis of policy content, with semi-structured interviews with policymakers and elected officials from state and local governments, to provide insights on the policy processes that are not otherwise revealed within the text of policies' contents. The following section presents the findings of this research.

Table 4.1 Policy analysis framework, adapting Transition Management elements

Strategic	Vision and objectives
	Green space goal
	Targets
	Green space definitions, functions and benefits
Tactical	Supporting strategies
	Partners (and community engagement)
Operational	Instruments and delivery mechanisms
Reflexive	Monitoring, evaluation and learning

4.4 Findings

4.4.1 Ecosystem Services and Associated Policy Domains

The urban ecosystem services typology (Gómez-Baggethun et al. 2013) was used as a basis for identifying relevant policy domains within which green space provision could potentially be addressed. The typology defines a comprehensive range of services and functions provided by urban green space, therefore underpinning a thorough identification of relevant policy domains. In applying this approach, we found that the planning and management of urban green space, as with other complex urban issues, is multilevel and cross-sectorial: all levels of government and multiple policy domains intersect with green spaces' provision of functions, services and benefits. In addition to urban land-use planning, which provides the overarching strategic directions for urban development and land use, other relevant policy domains include environmental sustainability, climate change, water, ecology and conservation, health and emergency management (Table 4.2).

These results reinforce understandings of green spaces' multifunctionality and the challenges for effectively providing urban governance approaches that will by necessity cross departmental and disciplinary boundaries (Fig. 4.1).

4.4.2 Policy Domains and Green Space Policies

All three levels of government have roles and policies associated with the policy domains identified. However, while green space's functions and roles may be relevant within these policy domains, not all of these policies necessarily address green space provision. The policies across the range of policy domains were reviewed to assess whether they included goals, targets, actions or other content that addressed green space provision.

We found that green space provision is most strongly addressed within the policy domains of *cities and urban planning, green space* and *climate change*, as well as *ecology and biodiversity*. Some policies within the *water* domain also address green space provision as part of integrated water management planning. For example, Victoria's recently released *Water for Victoria* has a chapter dedicated to 'Resilient and liveable cities and towns' that includes the action of 'improving stormwater management for greener environments' (p. 82). We found that health-related policies

Table 4.2 Urban ecosystem services and associated policy domains

Ecosystem service category and function	Associated policy domain
Provisioning	
Food supply	Health (public health: nutrition)
	Urban agriculture
Water supply	Water management: supply
Regulating	
Urban temperature regulation	Health (public health: heatwaves)
	Ecology and biodiversity
	Climate change
	Land-use planning
	Building regulations
Noise reduction	Environmental regulations (noise pollution)
	Land-use planning
Air purification	Environmental regulation (air pollution)
	Land-use planning
Moderation of climate extremes	Health (public health: heatwaves)
	Ecology and biodiversity
	Climate change
Runoff mitigation	Water management: drainage
	Land-use planning
Waste treatment	Environmental regulation (water pollution: waste management)
Pollination, pest regulation, seed dispersal	Urban agriculture
Global climate regulation	Climate change
Cultural services	
Recreation	Open space and recreation
	Health (public health: physical activity)
Aesthetic benefits	Open space and recreation
	Health (public health: physical and mental)
	Economic development
Cognitive development	Education
Place values and social cohesion	Health (public health: mental wellbeing)
	Community development and social welfare
Supporting	
Habitat for biodiversity	Ecology and biodiversity

rarely address green space provision, being largely focused on medical or disaster perspectives. While community wellbeing is addressed within the health policy domain, and there is growing recognition of the important role of green space for mental and physical wellbeing, few health domain policies then link to or integrate with policies for green space provision.

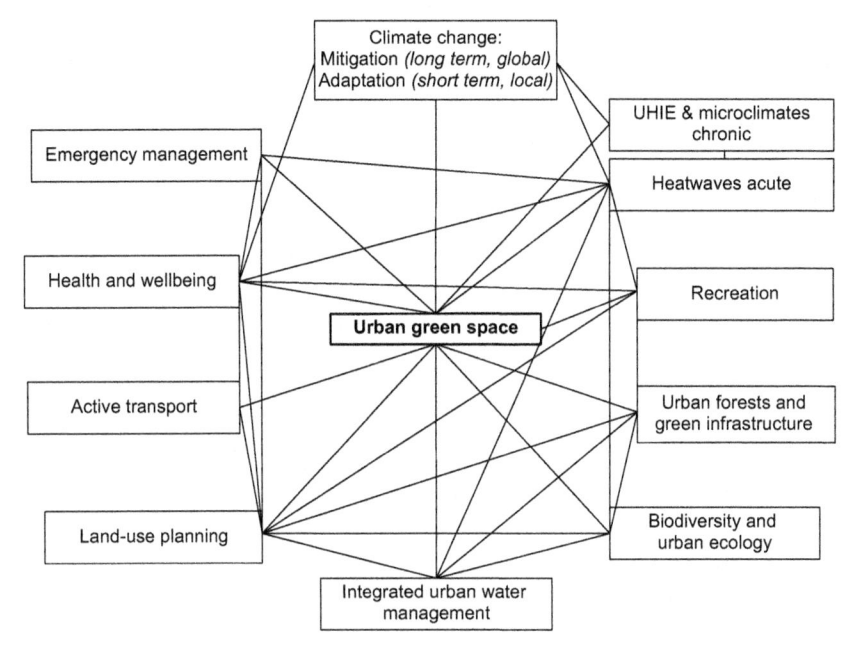

Fig. 4.1 Policy domains that address urban green space

4.4.3 Policies' Strategic, Tactical, Operational and Reflexive Elements

We applied the analysis framework (Table 4.1) to assess how policies from the domains of *cities and land use*, *green space* and *climate change* address the provision of urban green space. While the different levels of government, and even the different municipalities within the local government sector, have a range of different policy approaches, utilising different policy mechanisms, there were some common themes. We found that the *strategic* elements were most strongly and consistently addressed within the policies examined, and that *reflexive* elements were poorly addressed by most policies. Our analysis highlighted the key elements that underpin policies' contributions to retaining and maximising green space. These are highlighted below and discussed in the following section.

Strategic: Vision, Objectives and Targets
The analysis has found that while green space is often acknowledged within high-level, urban strategic plans, it is not a high-priority element, being addressed as one of many of the elements of the built form and community resources. Green space goals and targets are often framed as general aspirations.

Tactical: Alliances, Partnerships and Policy Integration
Tactical elements of supporting strategies and policy integration were generally poorly addressed with little integration between green space policies and the more influential land-use and transport policies. While a range of partners and alliances were identified across policies, there is a lack of linkages and shared objectives to underpin strong, ongoing, influential alliances and partnerships. In some cases, green space alliances and partnerships directly compete with each other when their specific green space focus is seen to be incompatible, for example between active recreation provision of sporting fields, biodiversity habitat and heritage landscapes.

Operational: Delivery Mechanisms
While strategies may list specific actions, there is often little detail on implementation responsibility, timing and funding. Without specific requirements and accountabilities, comprehensive implementation is not guaranteed. Furthermore, if additional funding provision is not committed, it is unclear how additional actions and responsibilities will be fulfilled or absorbed into existing responsibilities.

Reflexive: Monitoring and Evaluation
Evaluation of green space policies' implementation is not well addressed, with a lack of specification of processes, indicators and targets. In many cases it appears that evaluation is not undertaken, beyond the annual reporting required for government accountability. Furthermore, where data collection and analysis is undertaken, it is most commonly focused on quantitative indicators, and qualitative data and analysis are excluded from the 'evidence base' as 'anecdotal' and 'intangible'. As a result, services that are more difficult to assess, such as qualitative indicators and cultural elements are invisible, overlooked or ignored.

Green Space Policy Mechanisms
The mechanisms or instruments with which policies seek to achieve their aims and objectives can be categorised into four different types: government

provision or demonstration, information and engagement, incentives and awards, and regulations (Maddison and Denniss 2013). The policies analysed for this research utilise a range of policy mechanisms. Examples are provided in Table 4.3.

Table 4.3 Urban green space policy mechanisms

Policy mechanism type	Example
Government provision and demonstration	Install and maintain green space in public spaces Create parks from street closures or realignment Opportunistic public works (utilities/easements management) Water-sensitive urban design treatments integrated with street tree plantings Install green roof or other green space innovation on government-owned buildings
Information and engagement	Research and implementation partnerships: universities, peak bodies Community information, engagement, participation, including community plantings, citizen science, participatory planning and decision-making on green space design and implementation Guidelines, toolkits, seminar series, green roof tours: urban greening, green roofs, etc.
Incentives and awards	Incentives during the planning process: • Increased floor area ratios with increased green space provision • 'Green door' fast tracking of approvals for those which incorporate urban greenery features (e.g. green roofs, walls, open space, etc.) • Waiving planning fees • Exempt certain works related to urban green space Stormwater fee discount with increased pervious surfaces Grants, rebates, financing for installation of urban greenery features Awards and prizes
Regulations	Developer contributions (financial or land) for public open space Regulations, mandated for particular types of development, using Green Star model (Green Star Communities rating tool; ENV 3 UHI) Planning scheme overlays for 'hot spots' (based on temperature data): require specific heat mitigation treatments for private development Protection for heritage-listed trees Protection of public trees: penalties for damage

4.5 Discussion

Policies related to or affecting green space exist at all levels of government and across multiple policy domains and government departments. The policies utilise a range of policy mechanisms to address the policies' objectives and aims. Our analysis found that while multifunctionality is highlighted as a key benefit of urban green space provision, these multiple functions can also lead to policy fragmentation, duplication, lack of coordination and integration, and inconsistencies and contradictions in how green space is reserved and managed. This complexity also contributes to a lack of green space policy 'champions', arguably diffusing and weakening protection and enhancement offered by policy approaches. Based on our analysis, key 'success factors' associated with the development, endorsement and implementation of policies have been identified. In this section, the issues, challenges and opportunities for green space policies to contribute to the transition to eco-cities are discussed.

4.5.1 Policy Mechanisms for Transitions to Eco-Cities

The four different types of policy mechanisms address different intervention challenges and opportunities. *Government provision or demonstration* works to build the vision and shared narrative (and 'walk the talk'), as well as to support industry and skills development and experimentation. *Information and engagement* supports the development of knowledge, skills and expertise, and builds broader community support, which underpins continuing political support. *Regulations* set minimum standards, and *incentives* encourage and support innovation. In this way, policy mechanisms can calibrate implementation standards: regulations act to establish 'baseline' performance or practice, while incentives act to inspire efforts to best practice (Table 4.4). Furthermore, *regulations* by necessity are underpinned by an 'evidence base', while *incentives* act to create and test innovation for building an evidence base for increasingly ambitious policy.

The four types of policy mechanisms, understood and characterised in this way, can be conceptualised as part of transitions from the socio-technical systems of existing cities to the multifunctional social-ecological systems of eco-cities (Fig. 4.2).

As indicated in Fig. 4.2, government provision and demonstration and information and engagement can promote or push innovation, or alternatively can simply reinforce minimum, baseline standards, depending on their orientation in relation to the transition trajectory. (The curved lines

Table 4.4 Policy mechanisms and associated outcomes sought

Mechanism	Focus
Government provision or demonstration	Building a shared vision
	Development and demonstration of innovations, new approaches and technologies, industry skills and capacities
	Provision for public service
	Prioritisation to address inequities and vulnerabilities
Information and engagement	Support a shared vision and sense of urban green space stewardship
	Build broad-based skills
	Build and maintain political support
Incentives and awards	Foster ambition and innovation
	Encourage and support best practice
Regulations	Require compliance
	Define and enforce minimum standards

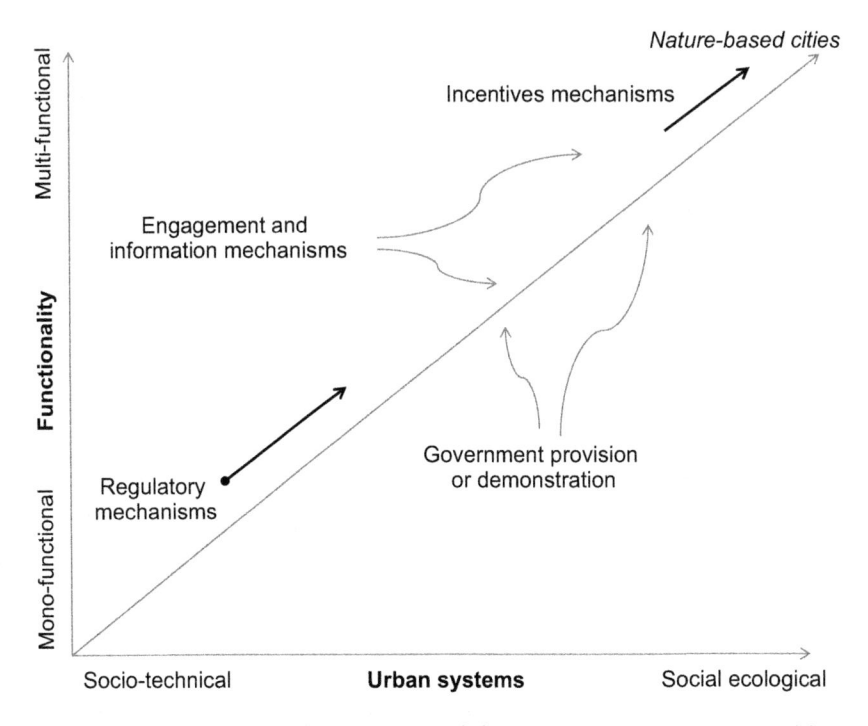

Fig. 4.2 Policy mechanism categories and the transition trajectory to eco-cities

symbolise the flexibility and potential responsiveness of the application of government provision and of engagement and information, while the straight lines reflect the relative rigidity of defined regulations and incentives programmes.) This reflects the different approaches that different governments bring to provision of green space, and green space policy approaches. Furthermore, while Fig. 4.2 represents the actions of policy mechanisms that promote and support transitions, in other cases, policy mechanisms may be set to hinder or resist transitions. For example, regulations may be set to define maximum provision or a ceiling on compliance, and incentives may be set to simply maintain standard practice and business-as-usual approaches.

4.5.2 Multifunctionality and Innovation

Our review of policies for urban green space found that green spaces' multifunctionality, encapsulated in the ecosystem services framework, creates opportunities for policies from across a range of domains to address green space provision. However this multifunctionality creates substantial challenges because governance structures, policy frameworks and implementation still largely operate in mono functional domains, budgets, departments and disciplines. There is a lack of integration and cross-referencing between the policies that do address green space provision. This lack of integration and cross-referencing further weakens the influence and operationalisation of specific policy approaches for green space. Furthermore, policy 'ownership' and championing of green space provision is potentially scattered across multiple government departments and jurisdictions, further diffusing influence and capacity.

Green space's multifunctionality is a key feature and engagement point across both research disciplines and government departments. While the multiple benefits are frequently highlighted as promoting and supporting action and efficient delivery of urban infrastructure needs, green space is usually understood by urban planners to be less 'efficient' at delivering single functions than the equivalent grey infrastructure (particularly, e.g. in the area of water management). Green space's health benefits are receiving increasing focus in research (van den Bosch and Ode Sang 2017; Davern et al. 2017) and in high-level strategic planning, but policies in the health domain largely do not address green space provision. At this stage, health policymakers have not yet actively engaged in green space policy development, hindered by potentially long-term timescales for delivery of health benefits, yet short-term timescales for budgets, delivery and measureable outcomes.

In addition, new forms of green infrastructure such as water-sensitive urban design treatments and green roofs and walls are in effect infrastructure innovations, in many cases lacking associated industry skills and knowledge related to installation, and maintenance requirements, techniques and costs. As such there is a risk, voiced by both researchers (e.g. Nesshöver et al. 2017; Clabby 2016) as well as some policy officers interviewed for this research, that the high expectations for 'green infrastructure' installations will not be met in practice. Furthermore, planners' and managers' assumptions that green infrastructure, utilising natural processes, will therefore require little or no ongoing maintenance further threaten both their ongoing performance, as well as perceptions of their efficacy in providing infrastructure roles. This has the potential to undermine the case for continuing installations, if perceptions grow that such installations are difficult or costly to manage.

Integration of green space into urban policy approaches epitomises the challenges of shifting to complex system thinking necessary for the transition to eco-cities. Although green space's multifunctionality is acknowledged, particularly within 'ecosystem services' and 'green infrastructure' framings, existing management approaches have only partially encompassed this multifunctionality. Funding and budgeting for urban green space presents challenges, with uncertainties in costs of ongoing maintenance of urban greening, particularly for new and innovative forms of green space such as green roofs and water-sensitive urban design treatments. Departmental funding, budgeting and reporting practices are not structured or equipped to effectively oversee multifunctionality and delivery of a range of services for a range of policy domains.

In addition, there is competition between and different priorities for urban greenings' range of functions or ecosystem services. Urban green space encompasses a wide range of different forms and functions; this research found that policy officers focus on delivery of the function consistent with their single, specific departmental priorities. For example, biodiversity officers focus on habitat provision, which may involve creating thick vegetation with high species diversity and dense understoreys. On the other hand, water managers focus on water-sensitive urban design treatments that could involve the use of only one or two species, planted to maximise water filtration and nutrient uptake. While these functions may be compatible with each other, it is not automatically the case, and there may be trade-offs between some functions and others, particularly if there is a lack of integration and communication between policy domains, government departments and green space planners and managers from across these areas. Advocacy and championing of specific, single green space functions leads to 'splintered narratives' and inward-facing competition, serving to diffuse and confuse coherent and united efforts for green space policy development, funding and implementation. Green space communications will be discussed in the following section.

4.5.3 Communications and Narratives

Translating a strategy or policy's vision into implementation requires commitment of resources for implementation. It also requires skills in shifting the narratives and business-as-usual methods of implementation, to redirect action towards new and integrated ways of delivering urban green space.

Communication, both within government departments as well as with broader community and stakeholders, is a key factor in policy uptake and implementation. A clear vision or 'narrative' that communicates green space's multifunctionality provides the impetus for implementation and the authorisation for uptake. While many of the policies assessed in this research provided strong statements of vision and goals for green space, the translation of these into tactical elements of building partnerships and community support (often requiring external communication) and organisational elements of redirecting implementation methods (requiring communication within the organisation) was less well developed.

Communicating with local residents and community groups poses challenges and difficulties for many of the policy officers interviewed. They reflected on the challenges caused in part by lack of training for community engagement and dealing with complaints, fear of conflict, and lack of organisational support or a clear and unambiguous organisational statement of vision for green space provision. On the other hand, some jurisdictions, in recognising the importance of communication, have invested in staff training and have developed clear, consistent communication, delivered across a range of channels and media, from interactive online maps to community breakfast workshops for urban forest precinct planning. As a result, staff members from these jurisdictions were more confident in addressing complaints. In addition, the active engagement and investment in a range of communication channels generated messages of positive feedback, including email love letters to individual street trees (CoM 2017), not just criticism and complaints.

Table 4.5 Policy success factors

Strategic	Leadership and champions
	Goals and targets
	Addressing splintered narratives
Tactical	Alliances and partnerships
	Community engagement
	Integration with other influential policies
Operational	Resources for implementation
	Range of policy mechanisms
	Technical skills
Reflexive	Monitoring and evaluation
	Peer-to-peer policy learning
	Indicator sets

4.5.4 Policy Success Factors

Analysis of the green space policies highlighted key policy success factors across the four dimensions of *strategic, tactical, organisational* and *reflexive*. These success factors include both organisational and individual characteristics (Table 4.5). Together, these factors contribute to increasing the adoption, implementation and ongoing support for the policies. Conversely, the lack of these factors was identified as contributing to poor outcomes or less effective implementation. The four dimensions reinforce the value of integrated policy approaches that operate at a range of levels (from *strategic*, long-term goals and visions to short-term *operational* resources for implementation), develop partnerships and reinforce the importance of monitoring and evaluation to underpin ongoing learning and policy development.

4.6 Conclusions: Transitions to Eco-Cities

The transition to eco-cities requires shifts from mono functional to multifunctional approaches to urban policies and to green space planning and management. We need to devise and experiment with new forms of governance that can encompass and embrace the multifunctionality of urban green space, as part of social-ecological systems in eco-cities. Currently most green space policy approaches have not yet developed to effectively address green space multifunctionality. Furthermore, policies for urban green space lack integration and influence compared with other urban policy domains particularly land-use planning and transport planning (Colding 2011; Mell 2017; Lindholm 2017). As cities strive to address environmental, social and economic challenges and transform towards eco-cities, policies for urban green space must be part of this transition. Underpinning this shift are the strategic, tactical, operational and reflexive elements of policies that together can support successful urban green space policy development and implementation.

4.7 Take-Home Tool and Approach: Twelve Success Factors for Effective Policies

Policy success—developing, endorsing and implementing policies that effectively contribute to urban green space provision—differs across jurisdictions and between cities, but common factors were identified. Conversely, the lack of these factors contributed to less effective implementation. These success factors include both organisational and individual characteristics (Table 4.5). The success factors are categorised according to the analytical framework's four dimensions: *strategic, tactical, organisational* and *reflexive*.

References

Benedict, Mark A., and Edward T. McMahon. 2006. *Green Infrastructure: Linking Landscapes and Communities*. Washington, DC: Island Press.

Birkeland, Janis. 2008. *Positive Development: From Vicious Circles to Virtuous Cycles Through Built Environment Design*. London: Earthscan.

Bosomworth, Karyn, Alexei Trundle, and Darryn McEvoy. 2013. *Responding to the Urban Heat Island: A Policy and Institutional Analysis*. Melbourne: Victorian Centre for Climate Change Adaptation Research.

Clabby, G. 2016. Delivering Green Infrastructure Through Planning: Insights from Practice in Fingal, Ireland. *Planning Theory and Practice* 17 (2): 289–295.

Cohen-Shacham, E., G. Walters, C. Janzen, and S. Maginnis. 2016. *Nature-Based Solutions to Address Global Societal Challenges*. Gland: IUCN (International Union for Conservation of Nature.

Colding, Johan. 2011. The Role of Ecosystem Services in Contemporary Urban Planning. In *Urban Ecology: Patterns, Processes, and Applications*, ed. Jari Niemelä, Jürgen H. Breuste, and Glenn Guntenspergen, 228–237. Oxford: Oxford University Press.

CoM. 2012. *Urban Forest Strategy. Making a Great City Greener. 2012–2032*. Melbourne: City of Melbourne.

———. 2017. *Nature in the City. Thriving Biodiversity and Healthy Ecosystems*. Melbourne: City of Melbourne.

Davern, M., A. Farrar, D. Kendal, and B. Giles-Corti. 2017. *Quality Green Public Open Space Supporting Health, Wellbeing and Biodiversity: A Literature Review*. Report prepared for the Heart Foundation, SA Health, Department of Environment, Water and Natural Resources, Office for Recreation and Sport, and Local Government Association (SA). Victoria: University of Melbourne.

Douglas, Ian, and Philip James. 2015. *Urban Ecology: An Introduction*. Abingdon, Oxon: Routledge.

EC. 2015. *Nature-Based Solutions and Re-Naturing Cities*. Final report of the Horizon 2020 Expert Group, Edited by European Directorate-General for Research and Innovation. Brussels: Directorate-General for Research and Innovation, European Commission.

Elmqvist, Thomas, Michail Fragkias, Julie Goodness, Burak Güneralp, Peter J. Marcotullio, Robert I. McDonald, Susan Parnell, Maria Schewenius, Marte Sendstad, Karen C. Seto, Cathy Wilkinson, Marina Alberti, Carl Folke, Niki Frantzeskaki, Dagmar Haase, Madhusudan Katti, Harini Nagendra, Jari Niemelä, Steward T.A. Pickett, Charles L. Redman, and Keith Tidball. 2013. Stewardship of the Biosphere in the Urban Era. In *Urbanization, Biodiversity and Ecosystem Services: Challenges and Opportunities. A Global Assessment*, ed. Thomas Elmqvist, Michail Fragkias, Julie Goodness, Burak Güneralp, Peter J. Marcotullio, Robert I. McDonald, Susan Parnell, Maria Schewenius, Marte Sendstad, Karen C. Seto, and Cathy Wilkinson, 719–746. Dordrecht: Springer.

Fainstein, Susan S., and James DeFilippis. 2016. *Readings in Planning Theory*. Chicester: John Wiley & Sons.

Frantzeskaki, Niki, Derk Loorbach, and James Meadowcroft. 2012. Governing Societal Transitions to Sustainability. *International Journal of Sustainable Development* 15 (1–2): 19–36.

Frantzeskaki, Niki, Julia Wittmayer, and Derk Loorbach. 2014. The Role of Partnerships in 'Realising' Urban Sustainability in Rotterdam's City Ports Area, the Netherlands. *Journal of Cleaner Production* 65: 406–417. https://doi.org/10.1016/j.jclepro.2013.09.023.

Geels, Frank W. 2002. Technological Transitions as Evolutionary Reconfiguration Processes: A Multi-Level Perspective and a Case-Study. *Research Policy* 31 (8–9): 1257–1274. https://doi.org/10.1016/S0048-7333(02)00062-8.

Geels, Frank W., and Johan Schot. 2007. Typology of Sociotechnical Transition Pathways. *Research Policy* 36 (3): 399–417. https://doi.org/10.1016/j.respol.2007.01.003.

Gómez-Baggethun, Erik, Åsa Gren, David N. Barton, Johannes Langemeyer, Timon McPhearson, Patrick O'Farrell, Erik Andersson, Zoé Hamstead, and Peleg Kremer. 2013. Urban Ecosystem Services. In *Urbanization, Biodiversity and Ecosystem Services: Challenges and Opportunities. A Global Assessment*,

ed. Thomas Elmqvist, Michail Fragkias, Julie Goodness, Burak Güneralp, Peter J. Marcotullio, Robert I. McDonald, Susan Parnell, Maria Schewenius, Marte Sendstad, Karen C. Seto, and Cathy Wilkinson, 175–251. Dordrecht: Springer.
Grimm, Nancy B., Stanley H. Faeth, Nancy E. Golubiewski, Charles L. Redman, Wu Jianguo, Xuemei Bai, and John M. Briggs. 2008. Global Change and the Ecology of Cities. *Science* 319 (5864): 756–760. https://doi.org/10.1126/science.1150195.
Lindholm, G. 2017. The Implementation of Green Infrastructure: Relating a General Concept to Context and Site. *Sustainability (Switzerland)* 9 (4). https://doi.org/10.3390/su9040610.
Loorbach, Derk. 2010. Transition Management for Sustainable Development: A Prescriptive, Complexity-Based Governance Framework. *Governance* 23 (1): 161–183. https://doi.org/10.1111/j.1468-0491.2009.01471.x.
Maddison, Sarah, and Richard Denniss. 2013. *An Introduction to Australian Public Policy: Theory and Practice.* 2nd ed. Port Melbourne: Cambridge University Press.
McPhearson, T., D. Haase, N. Kabisch, and Å. Gren. 2016a. Advancing Understanding of the Complex Nature of Urban Systems. *Ecological Indicators* 70: 566–573. https://doi.org/10.1016/j.ecolind.2016.03.054.
McPhearson, T., S.T.A. Pickett, N.B. Grimm, J. Niemelä, M. Alberti, T. Elmqvist, C. Weber, D. Haase, J. Breuste, and S. Qureshi. 2016b. Advancing Urban Ecology Toward a Science of Cities. *BioScience* 66 (3): 198–212. https://doi.org/10.1093/biosci/biw002.
MEA. 2003. *Ecosystems and Human Well-Being: A Framework for Assessment. Millennium Ecosystem Assessment.* Washington, DC: Island Press.
Mell, Ian C. 2012. Can You Tell a Green Field from a Cold Steel Rail? Examining the "Green" of Green Infrastructure Development. *Local Environment* 18 (2): 152–166. https://doi.org/10.1080/13549839.2012.719019.
———. 2017. Green Infrastructure: Reflections on Past, Present and Future Praxis. *Landscape Research* 42 (2): 135–145. https://doi.org/10.1080/01426397.2016.1250875.
MTPC. 1929. *Plan of General Development.* Edited by Metropolitan Town Planning Commission. Melbourne: Victorian Government, Metropolitan Town Planning Commission.
Nesshöver, Carsten, Timo Assmuth, Katherine N. Irvine, Graciela M. Rusch, Kerry A. Waylen, Ben Delbaere, Dagmar Haase, Lawrence Jones-Walters, Hans Keune, Eszter Kovacs, Kinga Krauze, Mart Külvik, Freddy Rey, Jiska van Dijk, Odd Inge Vistad, Mark E. Wilkinson, and Heidi Wittmer. 2017. The Science, Policy and Practice of Nature-Based Solutions: An Interdisciplinary Perspective.

Science of the Total Environment 579: 1215–1227. https://doi.org/10.1016/j.scitotenv.2016.11.106.

Register, Richard. 2006. *Ecocities: Rebuilding Cities in Balance with Nature*. Revised ed. Gabriola, BC: New Society Publishers.

Rotmans, Jan, Rene Kemp, and Marjolein van Asselt. 2001. More Evolution than Revolution: Transition Management in Public Policy. *Foresight* 3 (1): 15–31.

Trundle, A., and D. McEvoy. 2016. Urban Greening, Human Health, and Wellbeing. In *The Routledge Handbook of Urbanization and Global Environmental Change*, ed. Karen C. Seto, William Solecki, and Corrie Griffith, 276–292. New York: Routledge.

Turner, Tom. 2005. *Garden History: Philosophy and Design 2000 BC–2000 AD*. London: Taylor and Francis.

van den Bosch, M., and Å. Ode Sang. 2017. Urban Natural Environments as Nature-Based Solutions for Improved Public Health—A Systematic Review of Reviews. *Environmental Research* 158: 373–384. https://doi.org/10.1016/j.envres.2017.05.040.

Wolfram, M., and N. Frantzeskaki. 2016. Cities and Systemic Change for Sustainability: Prevailing Epistemologies and an Emerging Research Agenda. *Sustainability* 8 (2): 1–18. https://doi.org/10.3390/su8020144.

Xing, Y., P. Jones, and I. Donnison. 2017. Characterisation of Nature-Based Solutions for the Built Environment. *Sustainability (Switzerland)* 9 (1): 149. https://doi.org/10.3390/su9010149.

CHAPTER 5

Niches: Small-Scale Interventions or Radical Innovations to Build Up Internal Momentum

Andréanne Doyon

Abstract Niches act as small-scale interventions or radical innovations to build up internal momentum, which may lead to bottom-up change, or encourage major shifts within a system. Focusing on the niche experience offers a different way to understand and plan for eco-cities. This chapter offers an alternative approach to investigate eco-cities through niche interventions in the built environment. This is achieved by combining the fields of urban planning, resilience studies and sustainability transitions. In particular, panarchy from resilience studies and the s-curve and the multi-level perspective framework from sustainability transitions are brought together to explore changes within the built environment. This approach shows that incremental change is built from the existing system, and highlights the importance of timescales and pathways when planning for eco-cities.

Keywords Niches • Urban planning • Social-ecological systems • Sustainability transitions

A. Doyon (✉)
School of Global, Urban and Social Studies, RMIT University, Melbourne, VIC, Australia

© The Author(s) 2018
D. Hes, J. Bush (eds.), *Enabling Eco-Cities*,
https://doi.org/10.1007/978-981-10-7320-5_5

5.1 Introduction

The role of cities and the city-level scale has received increasing attention regarding climate change action (Betsill and Bulkeley 2007; Castán Broto and Bulkley 2013), and more broadly from sustainability transitions research (Hodson and Marvin 2009, 2010; Truffer and Coenen 2012; Hansen and Coenen 2015). Cities and urban regions generate great demands for resources, such as fresh water or clear air; they also generate large volumes of waste. At the same time, cities are hubs of service, knowledge, capital and innovation that can offer solutions to the challenges being faced (SRC 2014). Sustainable development and eco-cities have been part of the field of urban planning since the early 1990s (Low et al. 2005). More recently, cities, local governments and urban planners are increasingly interested in building more resilient cities (Sellberg et al. 2015), which support viewing cities as complex social-ecological systems.

This chapter proposes a new approach to urban planning for eco-cities. This is achieved by combining the fields of urban planning, resilience studies and sustainability transitions, and by investigating the role of niche interventions in the built environment. *Urban planning* supports the social and spatial transformation of cities by providing structure to space and human activity. Social-ecological *resilience*, or evolutionary resilience, interprets resilience as the ability of systems to adapt, change, or transform in response to shocks or stressors. *Sustainability transitions* are defined as co-evolutionary and non-linear transformations whereby innovations related to sustainability practices, policies, or technologies are adopted more broadly. This chapter is also responding to calls for more collaboration across different disciplines (Coaffee 2013; Elmqvist et al. 2014; Meerow et al. 2016). While there is a history of resilience and urban planning coming together (Davoudi 2012; Ahern 2013), urban planning and sustainability transitions are still underdeveloped.

The aim of this research is to investigate planning for eco-cities from the niche perspective, which offers an alternative way to examine cities. It contributes to understandings of urban change processes within the field of urban planning. Unlike incremental planning which aimed to solve existing problems, rather than planning ahead to achieve a desired state in future (Lindblom 1959), this paper applies social-ecological systems thinking to urban planning to contribute to understandings of eco-cities, as well as urban resilience, from the niche perspective. It does so by focusing on bottom-up change and innovations, rather than the whole system or a specific disturbance, and emphasising the importance of timescales and pathways in planning for urban resilience. New conceptualisations of urban resilience can provide opportunities for more progressive policies and niche interventions to support the planning for eco-cities.

This chapter begins by introducing the concept of the niche, before moving on to discussing the three bodies of literature: urban planning, resilience and sustainability transitions. This is done in three stages. First, the different literature is reviewed separately. Second, the literature is compared against each other. Third, elements of the different literature are combined to formulate new ways to conceptualise urban resilience. Next, the literature is applied through the development of a methodology. This chapter ends with a short discussion and conclusion.

5.1.1 Niches

The term niche originally comes from evolutionary biology, which uses "niche" to define an organism's role in a system. Of particular interest to this chapter are evolutionary niches (or niche construction), which refers to the process where an organism alters a system for its improvement or to increase its chance of survival (Oldling-Smee et al. 2003). From this perspective, niches act as small-scale interventions or radical innovations to build up internal momentum, which may lead to bottom-up change (Geels 2002; Smith 2007), or encourage major shifts within a system (Davoudi 2012). The term "niche" is also used in economics and business, where it is used to denote protected spaces, away from wilder environments or insulated from markets (Rip and Kemp 1998; Geels 2002). Markard and Truffer (2008) identified two types of niches: market niches and technology niches. Market niches are anomalies within the regime or system, while technology niches are deliberately created (Markard and Truffer 2008). A niche is also defined as "a discrete application domain (habitat) where actors are prepared to work with specific functionalities, accept such teething problems as higher costs, and are willing to invest in improvements of new technology and the development of new markets" (Hoogma et al. 2002, 4).

There is an emphasis on the role of niches and niche development in sustainability transitions research (Geels and Raven 2006) (discussed in more detail below). Within sustainability transitions research, niches have been identified as being able to "inform possibilities for developing more sustainable regimes' (Smith 2007, 429), which supports an evolutionary niche perspective. Rip and Kemp (1998, 381) argued that 'niches … are important for the further development of a new technology", which aligns with an economics perspective of niches. Many transitions' studies have traced the development of new regimes or systems to a particular niche (Geels 2005). Moving upward in the nested hierarchy of the multi-level perspective (MLP), niches may change the regime, and a new regime may change the landscape over the long term. The absence of structure and coordination at the niche level, compared to the regime and landscape, allows for new, agile interactions to take place that may support innovation. In strategic niche management (SNM), the focus is less on the movement of the niche through different levels but on creating protective spaces free of barriers for niches to develop before they interact with the regime. Similarly, transition management (TM) also aims to facilitate niche-based change; however, it is done through an iterative governance approach.

For this research, niche interventions refer to evolutionary or technology niches, a deliberately created niche to alter and improve the system. Niches come in the form of innovations, experiments, or bottom-up interventions, and may inspire change by building up internal momentum within a system (Geels 2002; Smith 2007; Grin et al. 2010).

5.2 Reviewing the Literature

This research intersects three academic fields: urban planning, resilience and sustainability transitions.

5.2.1 Urban Planning

Urban planning is the practice by which plans, programmes, and design are developed to intervene in the built environment (Healey 2010). Rather than have cities evolve randomly, urban planners set a course to move towards a goal, such as a more sustainable, resilient, compact, integrated, equal and just future. Urban planning is seen as both an object and a method (Fainstein and Campbell 2012). Urban planning is inherently complex—there is more than one objective (economic growth, fair distribution of income, social cohesion and stability, reduction of psychological stress, a beautiful environment, etc.), and the processes are multidimensional (Hall and Tewdwr-Jones 2011). As Rittel and Webber (1973, 136) contended, "planning problems are inherently wicked". To add to the complexity, different theories or approaches are chosen by planners for a myriad of reasons (conflicting pressures including personal/professional, place of work, location, professional body and education, amongst others), and sometimes different approaches are required for different circumstances (Allmendinger 2002).

Urban planning research investigates why planning exists and what it does, as well as how to go about it. As a field, it was established because of a need for effective government administration of land use and utilities (Fainstein and Campbell 2003). As a practice, it supports the social, spatial and environmental transformation of cities by providing structure to space and human activity (Hall and Tewdwr-Jones 2011). It can be seen as a method to manage space and human activity, or the practice "to connect forms of knowledge with forms of action in the public domain" (Friedmann 1993). At a more practical level, urban planning is responsible for granting approval of developments (Denyer-Green and Ubhi 2012). There are a number of mechanisms employed by local governments and urban planning departments to control land use. These include zoning, development controls, design guidelines and building codes, amongst others.

Earlier models of planning were based on scientific analysis, in an attempt to create some separation from politics (Friedmann 1987). Over time, more interactive and collaborative approaches were introduced that acknowledge different ways of thinking (Healey 2012), as well as greater understandings of environmental impact and sustainable development (Wheeler 2004). Different methods and mechanisms from urban planning have been developed to reduce their carbon output and develop in a more sustainable manner. They include "steering settlement away from flood-prone coastal areas and those subject to landslides; protecting forests, agriculture and wilderness areas and promoting new ones; and development and enforcing local climate change protection measures … Planning also plays a role in identifying hazard-prone areas and limiting their use through land-use zoning, tax incentives and the relocation of residents" (UNHSP 2009, 14).

More recently, there has been an interest in re-framing urban planning from the perspective of social-ecological systems (Porter and Davoudi 2012). As urban planning can play an important role in creating cities that support both social and ecological functions (Wong and Yuen 2011). As Wong and Yuen (2011, 3) state, eco-cities are comprised of "compact, pedestrian-oriented, mixed-use neighbourhoods that give priority to re-use of land and public transport" that provide "strong incentives not to use a car, [use] renewable energy and green tools to make the city self-sustaining".

5.2.2 Resilience

The term resilience comes from the Latin root *resilire*, meaning to spring back. Physical scientists were the first to use the term resilience to denote the characteristics of a metal spring, and describe the stability and resistance of materials to external shocks (Davoudi 2012). Since the 1960s, starting with ecologists and the rise of systems thinking, multiple concepts and meanings have been developed. These include disaster resilience, psychological resilience and military resilience, amongst others. The three most common forms of resilience within the built environment disciplines are engineering, ecological and social-ecological resilience.

Engineering resilience measures the gravity of a disturbance, and the speed with which the system returns to its previous state (Pimm 1991), and prefers technical or infrastructure-based solutions. Ecological resilience refers to the degree of disturbance that can be tolerated before the system changes its structure (Gunderson and Holling 2002). It rejects the notion of a single, stable equilibrium, recognising instead the existence of multiple equilibriums (Holling 1973). Social-ecological resilience, or evolutionary resilience, interprets resilience as the ability of systems to adapt, change, or transform in response to shocks or stressors (Carpenter et al. 2005). "This view of resilience reflects a paradigm shift in how scientists think about the world. Rather than seeing the world as orderly, mechanical and reasonably predictable, they see it as chaotic, complex, uncertain, and unpredictable" (Davoudi 2012, 302). From this perspective, resilience thinking provides a different, and useful, framework for problem-setting and problem-solving (Wilkinson 2011), and encourages working within a theoretical framework of multi-disciplinarity and multi-functionality (Ahern 2011).

From a social-ecological perspective, cities are understood to be complex, dynamic, multi-scale and adaptive systems (Davoudi et al. 2013; Elmqvist et al. 2014). By examining cities as social-ecological systems, the nuances and forces of change can be studied (Newman and Jennings 2008). Urban resilience, as defined by Alberti et al. (2003, 1170) (this definition is the most cited), is "…the degree to which cities tolerate alteration before reorganizing around a new set of structures and processes". Building urban resilience requires a diverse range of disciplines, perspectives and mechanisms, which brings together different approaches to explore viable pathways to transition to a resilient future (Coaffee 2013; Collier et al. 2013; Elmqvist et al. 2014; Meerow et al. 2016), as it is still a contested term (Leichenko 2011).

Resilience scholars have become increasingly interested in what is happening within cities, and planning scholars are concerned with how to build resilience. Resilience is believed to offer a number of benefits to the field of urban planning. These include working within an integrated social-ecological systems perspective (Ahern 2013); re-framing planning to include more fluid, reflexive, dependent, connected, multifaceted, interpretive and inclusive methods of planning (Davoudi and Strange 2009); and increasing the adaptive capacity of responses within cities (Wilkinson 2012). Urban planning may help resilience studies to define and critically assess urban resilience, as conceptualisations and examinations are varied.

5.2.3 Sustainability Transitions

A transition is a process of structural, non-linear system change in dominant practices (routines, behaviour, action), structures (institutions, economy, infrastructure) and cultures (shared values, paradigms, world views) that takes place over a period of decades (Rotmans et al. 2001; Grin et al. 2010). Sustainability transitions have been conceptualised as long-term processes of change and are the result of interacting economic, social, technological, institutional and/or ecological developments (Markard et al. 2012). The field of sustainability transitions focuses on the trajectory of change, and seeks to uncover the origins, patterns and mechanisms that drive these transitions. The multiphase concept, or the s-curve, represents the ideal transition, one where the system can adjust itself to changing internal and external dynamics (Grin et al. 2010), see Fig. 5.1.

The multi-level perspective (MLP), a core framework within sustainability transitions, offers an approach for investigating the processes by which innovations in socio-technical systems, arising in niches, displace

Fig. 5.1 The s-curve (adapted from Rotmans et al. 2001)

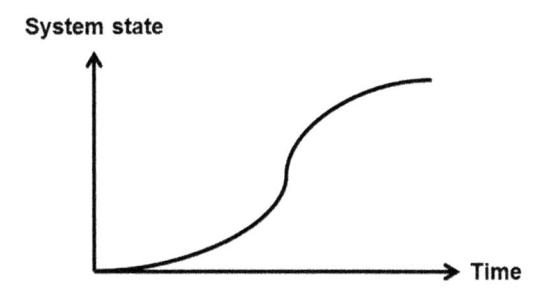

existing dominant or mainstream technologies. The MLP (Rip and Kemp 1998; Geels 2002) was first developed to explain technological transitions, and later socio-technical configurations (larger systems). Similar to structuration theory that seeks to explain the intersections between humans and wider systems and structures in which they are implicated (Giddens 1984), the MLP also emphasises and recognises the co-evolutionary nature of transitions (Twomey and Gaziulusoy 2014). As a framework, the MLP has a history of being adapted and added to (c.f. Geels and Schot 2007; Sangawongse et al. 2012; Geels 2014; amongst others). The MLP can be thought of as wireframe where different labels can be affixed to it, and additional components can be added to provide explanations. The evolutionary approach to studying transitions with the MLP, which favours niche pressure on the regime as a vehicle for transitions, provides a way to investigate a niche innovation within a system.

The MLP is divided into three levels that form a nested hierarchy: the landscape (macro level), the regime (meso-level) and the niche (micro-level) (Geels 2002); see Fig. 5.2. The nested character of the levels demonstrates that regimes are embedded within landscapes, and niches within regimes. Landscapes influence change both on niches and regimes; in return, niches (may) change the regimes and a new regime (may) change the landscape in the longer term.

Three strategies for changing regimes have been identified (Kemp et al. 2001). The first two strategies call for transformation at the landscape, through either altering the structure of incentives and permitting market forces to function or planning "for the creation and building of a new socio-technical system based on an alternative set of technologies" (Kemp et al. 2001, 279). The third strategy involves niches, and proposes to build

Fig. 5.2 Multi-level perspective as a nested hierarchy (adapted from Geels 2002)

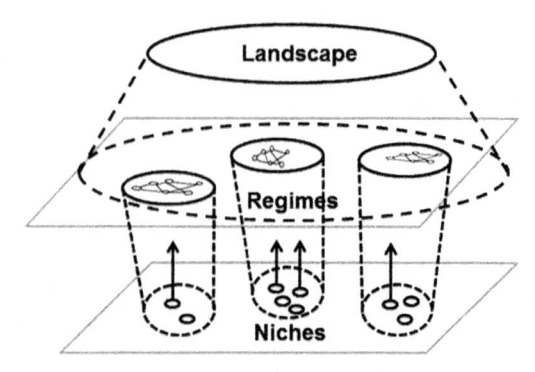

ongoing dynamics of change to exert pressure from the niches to influence transformations in desirable directions. The MLP is a useful framework for investigating Kemp et al. (2001) third strategy, niche evolution. The MLP is therefore useful to this research, because it is investigating niche interventions in the built environment.

5.3　Comparing the Literature

The following section compares the three bodies of literature: urban planning, resilience studies and sustainability transitions. Within the field of sustainability transitions, the role of cities and working at the city-level scale has received increasing attention. Work within the emerging theories of geography of transitions (Coenen and Truffer 2012; Hansen and Coenen 2015) and urban transitions (Hodson and Marvin 2009, 2010; Truffer and Coenen 2012; Hansen and Coenen 2015) has contributed to the field of sustainability transitions. This area of research seeks to increase the spatial and contextual aspects of transitions research, as well as the importance of the city and regional scale, and the role cities can play in transitions. The benefit of linking both approaches supports research for location-specific analyses of transition processes.

However, urban planning as a discipline has not received much interest from transition scholars, nor have urban planners engaged much with transitions research. "Transitions involve mutually coherent [cross-correlation] changes in practices and structures, and because of their multilayeredness and inevitable entrenchment in society and culture at large they are complex and comprehensive phenomena" (Grin et al. 2010, 3). Urban planning is also complex, with multiple objectives and multidimensional processes (Hall and Tewdwr-Jones 2011), which make planning problems inherently wicked. Sustainability transitions research is concerned with the capacity to accelerate and guide social innovation processes towards a more sustainable future (Loorbach and Rotmans 2010), and urban planning is about intervening in human settlements to achieve certain environmental, social, or political objectives (UNHSP 2009). Sustainability transitions and urban planning both share the desire to shape systems towards a specific normative goal. In the case of transitions, the orientation is sustainable development, and with urban planning, it is towards a better city (which includes objectives of sustainable development).

Resilience and urban planning has now developed as a stand-alone field of research. As resilience scholars have become increasingly interested in what is happening within cities, planning scholars are concerned with how to build resilience. However, the term resilience is still a relatively new concept within urban planning, as planners were not engaging with it before 2000 (Coaffee 2013). Resilience offers urban planning the opportunity to question its approach, and develop a more transformational and radical agenda, one that opens opportunities to challenge accepted ways of thinking (Porter and Davoudi 2012).

Research on sustainability transitions to date has focused on applying theories of sustainability transitions within a socio-technical conceptual framework. However, eco-cities are more suited to a social-ecological systems framework. There has been debate about the applicability of resilience to socio-technical systems and transformations to social-ecological systems, and the suggestion that application of the concepts cannot be interchanged between the two systems (Smith and Stirling 2010; Olsson et al. 2014). However, as Geels (2005) argued, social-ecological systems and socio-technical transitions do not separate humans from technology. Smith and Stirling's (2010) definition of social-ecological systems externalises technology, this research instead adopts the definition of social-ecological systems as "integrated living systems consisting of agents (human or otherwise), their actions and behavioural patterns, and a physical substrate (chemicals, energy, water)" (du Plessis 2009, 380). This definition supports Berkes and Folke's (1998) equal weighting of social and ecological, rather than the socio-technical perspective that views the social as a prefix to the technical, and not equal.

Other critiques against the applicability of resilience to address sustainability transitions discuss the bias towards adaptability and persistence in resilience, which is less suited for system transformations (Jerneck and Olsson 2008; Pelling and Manuel-Navarrete 2011). However, Olsson et al. (2014) argued that "resilience scholars do make a distinction between adaptation and transformation, and the mechanisms that reinforce a certain trajectory as well as support shifts from one trajectory to another" (no pagination). Transitions within the socio-technical perspective are often viewed within a nested hierarchy, such as the MLP (Geels 2002). From a social-ecological systems approach, complex adaptive systems are multi-scaled but not hierarchical (panarchy), meaning that adaptation at one scale might require or encourage transformation at another (Gunderson and Holling 2002; Folke et al. 2010; Olsson et al. 2014). Linking both approaches provides a way to analyse the transition process of niche innovations within a place-bound analytical unit, such as a city (Gallopín et al. 2001; Smith and Stirling 2010).

However, there have been scholars that have brought together TM with key resilience concepts such as adaptive management (AM) and adaptive governance (AG) to work within a social-ecological perspective. Foxon et al. (2009, 3) contend that by combining TM and AM together, "it may be possible to foster more robust and resilient governance of social–ecological systems than could be achieved by either approach alone". van der Brugge and van Raak (2007) argued that the multi-level framework, developed by Rip and Kemp (1998) (the precursor to the MLP), could be useful for AM research. First, the multi-level framework traces the evolution of a technology (or novelty) within the context of existing systems, regimes, strategic games and a slowly changing socio-technical landscape (Rip and Kemp 1998). Second, it can be used to uncover the different developments and scales, especially when used in a retrospective way (van der Brugge and van Raak 2007). Third, they believed the framework could help provide insights for management. Peter and Swilling (2014) highlighted key similarities between resilience and the MLP. Resilience conceptualises transitions through the adaptive cycle, and the MLP "can be influenced by self-organization (*i.e.*, adaptive capacity) and/or niche innovation (*i.e.*, creative capacity)" (Peter and Swilling 2014, 1602). Both theories view internal dynamics as uncertain, non-linear and having agency. However, as Hodson and Marvin (2010, 479) expressed "the MLP would benefit from additional development", this includes further investigation into conceptualising the MLP within the perspective of social-ecological systems.

5.4 Combining the Literature

Combining more than one distinct field of literature brings both benefits and challenges. Each field has its own disciplinary backgrounds, epistemology and ontology. Interdisciplinary research "involves occupying the spaces between disciplines to build *new* knowledge" (Davoudi and Pendlebury 2010, 638). This research is located within the recognised "highly interdisciplinary scientific field" (Wolfram and Frantzeskaki 2016, 143), known as studies of systemic change in cities. Within this field, Wolfram and Frantzeskaki (2016) have identified two established orientations: socio-technical systems and social-ecological systems. Urban planning and sustainability transitions are often located within a socio-technical systems perspective, while resilience is usually situated within social-ecological systems approach.

This research aims to bring together these three academic fields in a more integrated and explicit way. To date, the study of sustainability transitions has been dominated by socio-technical transition scholars and economists (Bernstein and Hoffmann 2015). Bernstein and Hoffmann (2015) claimed this presents an opportunity for those in other fields to contribute to theoretical innovations in the study of transitions. Comparatively, the field of resilience has been more diverse, and includes disciplines such as ecology and environmental sciences, biology, agriculture, social sciences, business and management, accounting, psychology, engineering and energy (Meerow et al. 2016). However, both fields do share certain gaps in their research or areas that would benefit from more explicit attention from urban planning scholars. Of particular relevance to this chapter are the interactions and combinations of urban planning, resilience and sustainability transitions.

While disciplines such as geography examine what happens within cities and why, urban planning uses this information to intervene and shape cities. There has been a movement to go beyond seeking innovative technological solutions to climate change, which include pursuing methods that include spatial planning and urban policy (Bruyninckx 2015). Integrating concepts and theories from urban planning highlights the role and scale of cities (Hodson and Marvin 2009, 2010; Truffer and Coenen 2012; Hansen and Coenen 2015), as well as the under-theorisation of governance, politics, and power (Shove and Walker 2007; Avelino and Rotmans 2009; Meadowcroft 2009) in resilience and transitions research.

However, urban planning can also learn from resilience and sustainability transitions. This chapter argues that urban planning would benefit from more experimentation and learning within its practices, as well as allowing more self-organisation to happen. The planning and creation of eco-cities should be framed around the cities' ability and capacity to positively adjust and adapt to change, as well as drive eco-city formation. Incorporating perspectives that focus on the process of change, and are associated with sustainability and resilience as the normative goal, may support calls for a re-framing of planning (Davoudi 2012). Studying the trajectory and acceleration of a niche intervention allows for further insight into understandings of planning for eco-cities.

This research contributes to the scholarship of sustainability transitions by proposing to rethink the systems in which transitions are studied. By investigating transitions within a social-ecological and resilience framework, rather than a socio-technical one, it moves the focus away from technology towards a more holistic and larger perspective. By extending transitions research to build understandings of transition processes at the city scale, this research offers a way to investigate alternative pathway trajectories of urban planning policies. Cities, regions and countries are complex social-ecological systems that include humans and their social and cultural institutions, as well as their infrastructures and built form. This re-framing may also be useful for conceptualising bigger issues such as climate change, politics and power and financial systems.

When it comes to ways to illustrate change, two approaches are useful for this research: the s-curve from sustainability transitions and the panarchy diagram from resilience studies (Fig. 5.3). The s-curve provides a useful method for studying historical change across different cases where differences in speed and acceleration are used to draw out different niche trajectories (Rotmans et al. 2001; Grin et al. 2010). When combined with a social-ecological perspective through the nested cycles of adaptive change (panarchy) (Gunderson and Holling 2002), there is a recognition that change is built upon what already exists. A socio-technical transition is viewed as a move into a better state, but within panarchy the better state is not permanent. Through the dynamic cycle of adaptive change, a new s-curve is produced to transition the niche or system into a new state. From this perspective, transitions would benefit from keeping some of the good elements of the existing system during a period of change.

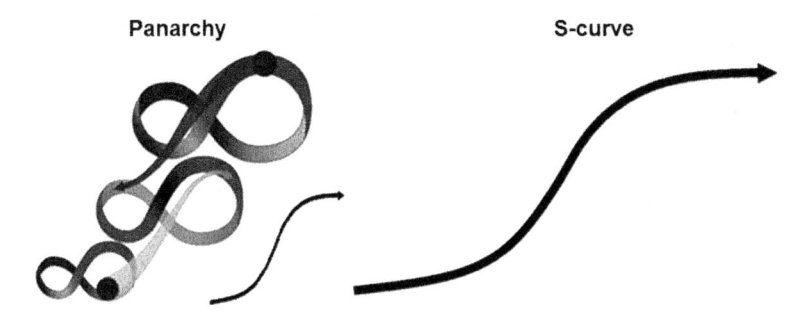

Fig. 5.3 Illustrations of change (adapted from Gunderson and Holling 2002)

Resilience studies understands change as being dynamic, such as through the cycle of adaptive change and panarchy. However, definitions or assessments of resilience and urban resilience are often viewed within a specific temporal frame. Drawing from this combination of panarchy and the s-curve in Fig. 5.3, this research's illustration of change is presented in Fig. 5.4. The application of the MLP from sustainability transitions to panarchy from resilience studies provides an alternative way to investigate planning for eco-cities through niche interventions. In Fig. 5.4, the MLP is placed within an x–y-axis, where the x-axis represents time, and the y-axis represents the system state. In this illustration, change is incremental, and is built from the existing system. The s-curve linking each system begins just below the regime level, where the niche and regime meet, and ends at the regime level in the new system. The position of the s-curve emphasises the role of the regime in niche interventions.

Situating this research within an urban planning field of inquiry elevates the role of cities in resilience and sustainability transitions, emphasises intervention in the built environment, and contributes to ways urban planning can support eco-cities. This research's application of sustainability transition theories to analyse policy innovation in social-ecological systems has demonstrated that the theories are relevant beyond the boundaries of socio-technical systems, and beyond solely singular or bifunctional technical innovation transition processes. A social-ecological resilience approach also supports the study of place-based sustainability transitions research. Frameworks from sustainability transitions offer different ways to explore eco-cities through the study of historical change. The speed and acceleration of events can trigger transitions and contribute to ways eco-cities are planned and investigated.

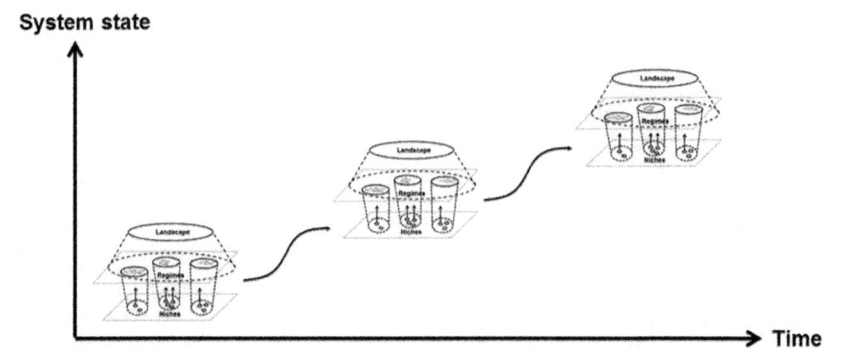

Fig. 5.4 Planning for eco-cities through niche interventions

5.5 Applying the Literature

This chapter proposes studying the trajectory of niche interventions to contribute to understandings of eco-cities. From sustainability transitions, the MLP is useful to this research because it can be used to track the trajectory of niches. Tracking the trajectory provides a structure to investigate how different cities have accepted new ways of thinking, and whether a more fluid and reflexive approach to urban planning can support eco-cities. To use the MLP as a way to investigate bottom-up change in cities, the three levels of the MLP were adapted to reflect an urban system: the landscape becomes the city, the regime urban planning, and niches vary depending on the city and context.

The city, as the landscape, is relatively static and cannot be easily changed by actors in the short term. The landscape embodies the physical, technical and material setting that supports the city as a system. The landscape level of investigation includes the overall setting and relevant history of each place. Within the context of this research, the regime is represented through urban planning (and government). Therefore urban planning, as the regime, is concerned with the structure, current practices, dominant rules (including zoning and building codes) and routines of the city. Niches can influence transformation and represent experimentation and innovation. Niches, as small-scale interventions and radical innovations, build up internal momentum, which may lead to bottom-up change. As mentioned previously, niches vary and can be any number of small-scale interventions in a city.

A social-ecological resilience approach supports the study of place-based sustainability transitions research. Resilience scholars have identified cities and urban regions as 'place-bound', natural analytical units to study the process of sustainability transitions (Gallopín et al. 2001; Pickett et al. 2003; Smith and Stirling 2010). Cities and urban regions can act as protected spaces to embed and diffuse niches and offer policies to stimulate certain industries. Panarchy acknowledges that regime shifts are not necessarily linear or the outcome of an external disturbance. Social-ecological resilience thinking believes that small-scale change can accelerate and amplify change to encourage major shifts in the system, and large intervention may have no or little effect (Davoudi 2012).

An example of studying a niche intervention in a city that led to subsequent niches is the introduction of different housing types in Vancouver from the 1980s, where each housing policy can be viewed as a niche. After artist protests in the mid-1980s, the City, in collaboration with local artists and architects, developed a series of relaxations on zoning and building codes to allow dwelling units in conjunction with artist studios. In 1995, the City responded by approving changes to permit non-artist live/work (City of Vancouver 1996) and established three different live/work types (artist, commercial and industrial) to respond to the increased interest. These changes coincided with the Living First Strategy (LFS), which created more housing in the central city, which included artist studios and live/work to support more people living and working in the central city. Now, more than 100,000 people call downtown Vancouver home. In 2008, the City launched their EcoDensity Charter, which aimed to increase density through invisible density (secondary-suites), hidden density (laneway houses) and gentle density (semi-detached and mixed-use housing). Secondary-suites and laneway houses existed prior to the Charter, but it provided a set of formal procedures and legality around these typologies. In 2009, under the fleeting Short Term Incentives for Rental (STIR) programme, Reliance Properties (local developers) used this opportunity to introduce micro-suites as a new housing typology in the city. What links these different policies together is the desire to increase density to provide more housing by developing or approving alternative housing options.

Each one of the housing types (live/work, secondary-suites, laneway houses, or micro-suites) has their own niche trajectory story. Each niche has its own experiences with the regime and landscape (governance structures, approaches to planning and different stakeholders), and we can learn from the different contexts that influence the progress of each individual niche. Studying each niche also contributes to the process of identifying and highlighting challenges and success factors in the adoption or failure (possibly only temporary) of niche interventions. When the trajectory of live/work as a niche was traced in the cities of San Francisco, Oakland, Vancouver and Melbourne, the research identified that rigid and top-down governance structures are less flexible and open to change, political approaches to urban planning are less responsive and adaptive, and strong political actors can either initiate or inhibit change. Meanwhile, collaboration and experimentation with technical skill can support the incubation and longevity of niche interventions (Doyon 2017).

Investigating the trajectory of multiple, consecutive niche interventions in one location can provide a more holistic understanding of a city's openness to small-scale interventions and radical innovations. By looking at niches together, and incorporating the MLP and social-ecological resilience in the analysis, we can learn more about the socio-political context and whether it is responsive to change and capable of adapting over time. Finally, this approach can help investigate whether the niches created positive ripple effects in a city, or if there potential for up scaling, diffusion, or mainstreaming of the niches.

5.6 Discussion and Conclusion

Urban planning plays an important role in creating and supporting eco-cities. Planning for eco-cities involves the integration of and thoughtful intervention in urban systems. It is rooted in long-term thinking, reflexivity, adaptability and flexibility. The investigation of planning for eco-cities is informed by niche interventions by directing the investigation of interventions in urban systems towards small-scale, bottom-up change. Focusing the study at the niche level brings the attention away from the whole system or a specific incidence (such as a disturbance or an event) to how the system reacts to small-scale or bottom-up changes. From this perspective, the capacity to support niche interventions (or evolutionary niches) may build up momentum and lead to positive alterations in cities. Or, as Davoudi (2012, 303) wrote, "small-scale changes in systems can amplify and cascade into major shifts".

Not all definitions of resilience or urban resilience have a temporal element, but for those that do, the focus is normally on the speed of recovery from a disturbance, shock, or stress to the system. A rapid recovery is often associated with an engineering or single-state equilibrium approach. Timescale is more complicated when resilience has multiple or non-equilibrium. The use of sustainability transitions extends the timescale discussion by considering resilience over time and not just a single disturbance or change. Rather than ask how quickly the city bounced back after a disaster, we should be asking how the city can respond to different internal and external shocks and stressors over time.

This research was interested in conceptualising the process of change within cities, in particular, the experience of niche interventions in planning for eco-cities. Rather than focus on the entire system, or a specific disturbance, this research sought to develop an approach to track the trajectory of a niche intervention. With the aim to be able to uncover ways in which different cities support (or inhibit) planning for eco-cities. This research has shown that combing urban planning, resilience, and sustainability transitions with a focus on niche interventions provides an alternative way to both investigate and understand eco-cities. The application of the approach demonstrates that investigating eco-cities from the perspective of a niche intervention brings new insights into how a city, and its approach to urban planning, supports eco-cities. By allowing innovations to incubate and amplify, and build its capacity to constructively move, adapt and change, new learnings are gained on how a city operates and responds to internal and external pressures.

This chapter contributes to debates in the literature by situating resilience and sustainability transitions research at the city scale, and by increasing the attention given to the role of cities. This research has proposed combining the fields of urban planning, resilience and sustainability transitions to contribute to conceptualisations of eco-cities. As well as each field offering particular insights to the other fields of inquiry. Such as urban planning emphasising intervention, resilience viewing cities through a social-ecological, complex adaptive systems approach, and sustainability transitions investigating non-linear change over time.

5.7 Take-Home Tool and Approach: Niche Interventions and Innovations

- Embrace complexity and accept that change is non-liner.
- Planning as a practice would benefit from more experimentation.
- Think of niches as opportunities to intervene in the system through small-scale experiments.
- Without risk there is no reward. Use niche interventions as an opportunity to learn about the system. Successes and failures provide insight to the system.
- Multiple niches provide an opportunity for a more holistic understanding of the system, and supports alternative pathways to plan for eco-cities.

References

Ahren, Jack. 2011. From Fail-Safe to Safe-to-Fail: Sustainability and Resilience in the New Urban World. *Landscape and Urban Planning* 100: 341–343.

Ahern, Jack F. 2013. Urban Landscape Sustainability and Resilience: The Promise and Challenges of Integrating Ecology with Urban Planning and Design. *Landscape Ecology* 28 (6): 1203–1212.

Alberti, Marnia, John M. Marzluff, Eric Shulenberger, Gordon Bradley, Clare Ryan, and Craig Zumbrunnen. 2003. Integrating Human Into Ecology:

Opportunities and Challenges for Studying Urban Ecosystems. *BioScience* 53 (12): 1169–1179.
Allmendinger, Philip. 2002. *Planning Theory.* New York: Palgrave.
Avelino, Flor, and Jan Rotmans. 2009. Power in Transition: An Interdisciplinary Framework to Study Power in Relation to Structural Change. *European Journal of Social Theory* 12 (4): 543–569.
Berkes, Fikret, and Carl Folke. 1998. *Linking Social and Ecological Systems: Management Practices and Social Mechanisms for Building Resilience.* Cambridge: Cambridge University Press.
Berstein, Steven, and Matthew Hoffman. 2015. *The Politics of Decarbonization: A Framework and Method.* Toronto: Environmental Governance Lab, University of Toronto.
Betsill, Michelle, and Harriet Bulkeley. 2007. Looking Back and Thinking Ahead: A Decade of Cities and Climate Change Research. *Local Environment* 12 (5): 447–456.
Bruyninckx, Herman. 2015. *Sustainability Transitions and EU Policy.* Presented at International Sustainability Transitions Conference 2015, Sustainability Transitions Research Network.
Carpenter, Stephen R., Frances Westley, and Monica G. Turner. 2005. Surrogates for Resilience of Social-Ecological Systems. *Ecosystems* 8 (8): 941–944.
Castán Broto, Vaness, and Harriet Bulkeley. 2013. A Survey of Urban Climate Change Experiments in 100 Cities. *Global Environmental Change* 23 (1): 92–102.
City of Vancouver. 1996. *Live/Work and Work/Live: Vancouver Overview Including Strategic Directions.* Vancouver, BC: City of Vancouver.
Coaffee, J. 2013. Towards Next-Generation Urban Resilience in Planning Practice: From Securitization to Integrated Place Making. *Planning Practice and Research* 28 (3): 323–339.
Coenen, Lars, and Bernard Truffer. 2012. Places and Spaces of Sustainability Transitions: Geographical Contributions to an Emerging Research and Policy Field. *European Planning Studies* 20 (3): 367–374.
Collier, Marcus J., Zorica Nedović-Budić, Jeron Aerts, Stuart Connop, Dermot Foley, Karen Foley, Darryl Newport, Siobhan McQuaid, Aleksander Slaev, and Peter Verburg. 2013. Transitioning to Resilience and Sustainability in Urban Communities. *Cities* 32: 521–528.
Davoudi, Simin, and Ian Strange. 2009. *Conceptions of Space and Place in Strategic Spatial Planning.* London: Routledge.
Davoudi, Simin, and John Pendlebury. 2010. Centenary Paper: The Evolution of Planning as an Academic Discipline. *Town Planning Review* 81 (6): 613–646.
Davoudi, Simin. 2012. Resilience: A Bridging Concept or a Dead End? "Reframing". *Planning Theory and Practice* 13 (2): 299–307.

Davoudi, Simin, Elizabeth Brooks, and Abid Mehmood. 2013. Evolutionary Resilience and Strategies for Climate Adaptation. *Planning, Practice and Research* 28 (3): 307–322.
Denyer Green, Barry, and Navjit Ubhi. 2012. *Development and Planning Law.* Hoboken: Taylor and Francis.
Doyon, Andréanne. 2017. Emerging Theoretical Space: Urban Planning and Sustainability Transitions. In *Urban Sustainability Transitions: Australian Cases—International Perspectives*, ed. Trivess Moore, Fjalar J. de Haan, Ralph Horne, and Brendan J. Gleeson. Singapore: Springer.
du Plessis, Chrisna. 2009. *An Approach to Studying Urban Sustainability from within an Ecological Worldview.* Doctoral thesis, University of Salford.
Elmqvist, Thomas, Guy Barnett, and Cathy Wilkinson. 2014. Exploring Urban Sustainability and Resilience. In *Resilient Sustainable Cities: A Future*, ed. Peter Roberts, Peter Newton, and Leonie Pearson, 19–28. New York: Routledge.
Fainstein, Susan, and Scott Campbell. 2003. *Readings in Planning Theory.* 2nd ed. Hoboken: Blackwell Publishing.
———. 2012. *Readings in Planning Theory.* 3rd ed. Hoboken: Blackwell Publishing.
Folke, Carl, Stephen R. Carpenter, Brian Walker, Marten Scheffer, Terry Chapin, and Johan Rockstörn. 2010. Resilience Thinking: Integrating Resilience, Adaptability and Transformability. *Ecology and Society* 15 (4): 20.
Foxon, Timothy J., Mark S. Reed, and Lindsay C. Stringer. 2009. Governing Long-Term Social-Ecological Change: What Can the Adaptive Management and Transition Management Approaches Learn from Each Other? *Environmental Policy and Governance* 19 (1): 3–20.
Friedmann, John. 1987. *Planning in the Public Domain: From Knowledge to Actions.* Princeton: Princeton University Press.
———. 1993. Toward a Non-Euclidian Mode of Planning. *Journal of the American Planning Association* 59 (4): 482–485.
Gallopín, Gilberto C., Silvio Funtowicz, O'Conner Martin, and Jerry Ravetz. 2001. Science for the Twenty-First Century: From Social Contract to the Scientific Core. *International Social Science Journal* 53 (168): 219–229.
Geels, Frank W. 2002. Technological Transitions as Evolutionary Reconfiguration Processes: A Multi-Level Perspective and a Case-Study. *Research Policy* 31 (8–9): 1257–1274.
———. 2005. The Dynamics of Transitions in Socio-Technical Systems: A Multi-Level Analysis of the Transition Pathway from Horse-Drawn Carriages to Automobiles (1860–1930). *Technology Analysis and Strategic Management* 17 (4): 445–476.
Geels, Frank W., and Rob Raven. 2006. Non-Linearity and Expectations in Niche-Development Trajectories: Ups and Downs in Dutch Biogas Development (1973–2003). *Technology Analysis and Strategic Management* 18 (3–4): 375–392.

Geels, Frank W., and Johan Schot. 2007. Typology of Sociotechnical Transition Pathways. *Research Policy* 36 (3): 399–417.

Geels, Frank W. 2014. Regime Resistance Against Low-Carbon Transitions: Introducing Politics and Power into the Multi-Level Perspective. *Theory, Culture and Society* 31 (5): 1–20.

Giddens, Anthony. 1984. *The Constitution of Society: Outline of the Theory of Structuration*. Oxford: Polity Press.

Grin, John, Jan Rotmans, and Johan Schot. 2010. *Transitions to Sustainable Development: New Directions in the Study of Long Term Transformative Change*. New York: Routledge.

Gunderson, Lamce H., and C.S. Holling. 2002. *Panarchy: Understanding Transformations in Human and Natural Systems*. New York: EandFN Spon.

Hall, Perter, and Mark Tewdwr-Jones. 2011. *Urban and Regional Planning*. 5th ed. London: Routledge.

Hansen, Teis, and Lars Coenen. 2015. The Geography of Sustainability Transitions: Review, Synthesis and Reflections on an Emergent Research Field. *Environmental Innovation and Societal Transitions* 17: 92–109.

Healey, Patsy. 2010. In Search of the "Strategic" in Spatial Strategy Making. *Planning Theory & Practice* 10 (4): 439–457.

———. 2012. Traditions of Planning Thought. In *Readings in Planning Theory*, ed. Susan Fainstein and Scott Campbell. Hoboken: Wiley-Blackwell.

Hodson, Mike, and Simon Marvin. 2009. Cities Mediating Technological Transitions: Understanding Visions, Intermediation and Consequences. *Technology Analysis and Strategic Management* 21 (4): 515–534.

———. 2010. Can Cities Shape Socio-Technical Transitions and How Would Know if They Were? *Research Policy* 39: 477–485.

Holling, C.S. 1973. Resilience and Stability of Ecological Systems. *Annual Review of Ecology and Systematics* 4: 1–23.

Hoogma, Remco, Rene Kemp, Johan Schot, and Bernard Truffer. 2002. *Sustainable Transport: The Approach of Strategic Management*. London: Spon Press.

Jerneck, Anne, and Lennart Olsson. 2008. Adaptation and the Poor: Development, Resilience and Transition. *Climate Policy* 8 (2): 170–182.

Kemp, Rene, Arie Rip, and Johan Schot. 2001. Constructing Transition Paths Through the Management of Niches. In *Path Dependence and Creation*, ed. Raghu Garud and Peter Karnøe, 269–299. London: Lawrence Erlbaum Associates.

Leichenko, Robin. 2011. Climate Change and Urban Resilience. *Current Opinion in Environmental Sustainability* 3 (3): 164–168.

Lindblom, Charles E. 1959. The Science of "Muddling Through". *Public Administration Review* 19 (2): 79–88.

Loorbach, Derk, and Jan Rotmans. 2010. The Practice of Transition Management: Examples and Lessons from Four Distinct Cases. *Futures* 42 (3): 237–246.

Low, Nicholas, Brendan Gleeson, and Darko Radovic. 2005. *The Green City, Sustainable Homes, Sustainable Suburbs*. London: Routledge.

Markard, Jochen, and Bernard Truffer. 2008. Technological Innovation Systems and the Multi-Level Perspective: Towards an Integrated Framework. *Research Policy* 37 (4): 596–615.

Markard, Jochen, Rob Raven, and Bernard Truffer. 2012. Sustainability Transitions: An Emerging Field of Research and Its Prospects. *Research Policy* 41 (6): 955–967.

Meadowcroft, James. 2009. What About the Politics? Sustainable Development, Transition Management, and Long Term Energy Transitions. *Policy Sciences* 42 (4): 323–340.

Meerow, Sara, Joshua P. Newell, and Melissa Stults. 2016. Defining Urban Resilience: A Review. *Landscape and Urban Planning* 147: 38–49.

Newman, Peter, and Isabella Jennings. 2008. *Cities and Sustainable Ecosystems: Principals and Practices*. Washington: Island Press.

Odling-Smee, John, Kevin N. Laland, and Marcus W. Feldman. 2003. *Niche Construction: The Neglected Process in Evolution*. Princeton: Princeton University Press.

Olsson, Per, Victor Galaz, and Wiebren J. Boonstra. 2014. Sustainability Transformations: A Resilience Perspective. *Ecology and Society* 19 (4): 1.

Pelling, Mark, and David Manuel-Navarrete. 2011. From Resilience to Transformation: Adaptive Cycle in Two Mexican Urban Centers. *Ecology and Society* 16 (2): 11.

Peter, Cameren, and Mark Swilling. 2014. Linking Complexity and Sustainability Theories: Implications for Modelling Sustainability Transitions. *Sustainability* 6 (3): 1594–1622.

Pickett, Steward T.A., Mary L. Cadenasso, and Tracy L. Benning. 2003. Biotic and Abiotic Variability as Key Determinants of Savannah Heterogeneity at Multiple Spatiotemporal Scales. In *The Kruger Experience: Ecology Management of Savannah Heterogeneity*, ed. Johan T. Du Toit, Kevin H. Rogers, and Harry C. Biggs, 22–40. Washington: Island Press.

Pimm, Stuart L. 1991. *The Balance of Nature? Ecological Issues in the Conservation of Species and Communities*. Chicago: University of Chicago Press.

Porter, Libby, and Simin Davoudi. 2012. The Politics of Resilience for Planning: A Cautionary Note. *Planning Theory and Practice* 13 (2): 329–333.

Raven, Rob Raven, Suzanne van Der Bosch, and Rob Waterings. 2010. Transitions and Strategic Niche Management: Towards a Competence Kit for Practitioners. *International Journal of Technology Management* 51 (1): 57–74.

Rip, Arie, and Rene Kemp. 1998. Technological Change. In *Human Choices and Climate Change*, ed. Steve Rayner and Elizabeth L. Malone, vol. II, 327–399. Columbus: Battelle Press.

Rittel, Horst W.J., and Melvin M. Webber. 1973. Dilemmas in a General Theory of Planning. *Policy Sciences* 4: 155–169.

Rotmans, Jan, Rene Kemp, and Marjolein Van Asselt. 2001. More Evolution than Revolution: Transition Management in Public Policy. *Foresight* 3 (1): 15–31.

Sangawongse, Somporn, Frans Senger, and Rob Raven. 2012. The Multi-Level Perspective and the Scope for Sustainable Land Use Planning in Chiang Mai City. *Environment and Natural Resources Journal* 10 (2): 21–30.

Sellberg, My M., Cathy Wilkinson, and Gary D. Peterson. 2015. Resilience Assessment: A Useful Approach to Navigate Urban Sustainability Challenges. *Ecology and Society* 20 (1): 43.

Shove, Elizabeth, and Gordan Walker. 2007. CAUTION! Transitions Ahead: Politics, Practice, and Sustainable Transition Management. *Environment and Planning A* 39 (4): 763–770.

Smith, Adrian. 2007. Translating Sustainabilities Between Green Niches and Socio-Technical Regimes. *Technology Analysis and Strategic Management* 19 (4): 427–450.

Smith, Adrian, and Andy Stirling. 2010. The Politics of Social-Ecological Resilience and Sustainable Socio-Technical Transitions. *Ecology and Society* 15 (1): 11.

Stockholm Resilience Centre. 2014. What is Resilience? Accessed August 29, 2017. http://www.stockholmresilience.org/download/18.10119fc11455d3c557d6d21/1459560242299/SU_SRC_whatisresilience_sidaApril2014.pdf.

Truffer, Bernard, and Lars Coenen. 2012. Environmental Innovation and Sustainability Transitions in Regional Studies. *Regional Studies* 46 (1): 1–21.

Twomey, Paul, and Idil Gaziulusoy. 2014. *Review of System Innovation and Transitions Theories*. Accessed August 29, 2017. http://www.visionsandpathways.com/wp-content/uploads/2014/10/Gaziulusoy_Twomey_NewBusinessModels.pdf.

United Nations Human Settlements Programme [UN Habitat]. 2009. *Planning Sustainable Cities: Global Report on Human Settlements*. London: Earthscan.

van der Brugge, Rutger, and Roel van Raak. 2007. Facing the Adaptive Management Challenge: Insights from Transition Management. *Ecology and Society* 12 (2): 33.

Wheeler, Stephen M. 2004. *Planning for Sustainability, Creating Livable, Equitable, and Ecological Communities*. London: Routledge.

Wilkinson, Cathy. 2011. Strategic Navigation: In Search of an Adaptable Mode of Strategic Spatial Planning Practice. *Town Planning Review* 82 (5): 595–613.

———. 2012. Urban Resilience: What Does it Mean in Planning. *Planning Theory and Practice* 13 (2): 319–324.

Wolfram, Marc, and Niki Frantzeskaki. 2016. Cities and Systemic Change for Sustainability: Prevailing Epistemologies and an Emerging Research Agenda. *Sustainability* 8: 1–13.

Wong, Tai-Chee, and Belinda Yuen. 2011. *Eco-City Planning: Policies, Practice and Design*. Dordrecht: Springer Science and Business Media.

CHAPTER 6

Benefit Driven Design Process: An Inclusive and Transdisciplinary Approach Towards Enabling More Resilient and Thriving Outcomes

Angelica Rojas-Gracia

Abstract Around the world there is an increasing number of projects that use the design process to co-create outcomes beyond the provision of physical infrastructure. This chapter explores the role of the design process in supporting developments embedded in social-ecological systems (SES). Two case studies are presented as precedents to explore the Benefit Driven Design Process (BDDP). BDDP is a set of activities that recognise and use their 'regenerative' and 'transformational' capacity to support collective and individual actions towards more inclusive, resilient and beneficial interactions between the systems that converge in a project. The enabling activities identified in the case studies are then applied and adapted to a project in Nepal. The chapter concludes by discussing the potential of applying BDDPs towards the development of eco-cities.

Keywords Design process • Mediators • Social-ecological system
• Regenerative development • Participation

A. Rojas-Gracia (✉)
Thrive Research Hub, Faculty of Architecture, Building and Planning,
The University of Melbourne, Parkville, VIC, Australia

6.1 Introduction

An eco-city is a city that works with its ecosystems, to minimise its impacts and to maximise its ability to support all beings to thrive. That is, it is a city that evolves to work within a living social-ecological system, which is an understanding of the city and its embedded scales as an ecosystem—an interdependent, nested, complex, dynamic and unpredictable system 'we' are all interconnected with and dependant on. How does the design process fit within this approach?

This chapter reflects on the role of the design process in supporting social-ecological systems (SES) which are 'integrated system[s] of people and nature with reciprocal feedback and interdependence' (Stockholm Resilience Center 2014, 18). Despite the multiple efforts to embrace a more 'sustainable' approach to design and development, the negative impacts of the built environment on the social-ecological system are growing. The complexity of the interconnected 'wicked' challenges that the world faces today such as climate change, social and ecological injustice and so forth requires not only new ways of thinking. It also demands ways to stimulate collective discussion, dialogue and action towards the construction and co-creation of a thriving, if different shared future.

Design processes, understood as interconnected nodes of interactions, are well placed to provide a medium for this co-creation. Design processes are inherently future thinking and generally look to connect to the larger system. Around the world there is an increasing number of projects that use the design process to co-create outcomes that provide benefits beyond the provision of physical infrastructure. This research presents two case studies as precedents to explore the Benefit Driven Design Process (BDDP), a set of activities that recognise and use their 'regenerative' and 'transformational' capacity to support the SES. Rather than seeing design processes as endeavours to 'produce' buildings or any form of physical space, they are understood as active 'mediators' and 'enablers' that provide the fertile 'grounds' to stimulate collective and individual actions towards more adaptive, inclusive, resilient and beneficial interactions between the flows that converge in a project. The lessons from the case studies are then applied and adapted to a project in Nepal, to a school devastated by the 2015 earthquakes. This chapter presents research that explores the role of the design processes through an iterative methodology that combines heuristic, case study and research by project methods.

6.2 Methods

The research uses an iterative practice-focused approach that combines case study (Yin 2014), design research (Downton 2013; Allpress et al. 2012) and heuristic (Moustakas 1990) research methods. Following a desktop review of 40 projects, two learning facilities were selected as case studies. The two case studies directly address socio-economic inequality and primarily focus on child development. They also have ecological imperatives included as a significant part of the design agenda. Both projects' design processes involved participation and engagement of the local communities. Data for the case studies was collected through fieldwork, documentation, open dialogues, semi-structured interviews and reflection. The data was analysed through pattern identification methods with the research questions in mind.

Analysis of the case studies identified a set of enabling activities that expand the capabilities of design processes towards the creation of potential benefits that support the development of vitality, viability and resilience (Mang and Haggard 2016). These activities were then applied and adapted to the school rebuilding project in rural Nepal through a process of design research where the researcher was also part of the design team. For over a year the researcher led a collaborative design process for the school, testing the Benefit Driven Design Process and applying regenerative development principles with the aim to enable positive contributions intertwined with the creation of the physical infrastructure.

The research focused on the expanding capabilities of design processes and the enabling activities that can be used to underpin such expansion. The research did not include all the aspects involved in design but only those key actions or processes that enable or enhance benefits beyond the spatial outcomes. Whilst the research also provided a reflection on disenabling processes found in the case studies, these are not discussed in this chapter due to space constraints.

6.3 Results: The Case Studies and Their Enabling Activities

This section presents the two case studies and summarises the enabling activities that harnessed the capabilities of these projects to support their local communities and ecosystems. The research investigated the links between actions or processes during the design that created 'benefits' beyond the provision of physical infrastructure. The research drew from documents and interviews to identify benefits and then investigated the enabling activities used to boost beneficial interactions and outcomes.

6.3.1 Case Study 1: The Venny, Kensington, Melbourne, Australia

Background
The Venny is a community facility that offers a place after school for children between 5 and 16 years old from the Kensington public housing estate and surrounding areas. Based on the philosophy that it is 'better a broken bone than a broken spirit', the Venny embraces a resilient approach to risk, balancing the need for freedom and protection (Gill 2007). It provides the conditions for children to engage in supervised and unstructured risk-taking play, which is considered vital to develop decision-making and social skills (Our Community Pty Ltd 2014). 'This play is designed by children, and led by children' (von der Borch 2011, 6). They are encouraged to create their own play dynamics through exploration, negotiation with others and direct manipulation and engagement with their space, climbing trees and altering spatial structures for different forms of play.

The Design Process
The programme operated for 30 years in an old bunker-like building, located on land owned by the local government, City of Melbourne (CoM). When the Venny's manager approached CoM seeking support for the programme, a building assessment revealed that the facility needed to be demolished due to a series of occupational health and safety (OHS) issues including asbestos, structural degradation and land contamination. CoM agreed to design and build a new purpose-built facility.

Though the idea of a new building was appealing to staff, it was not initially embraced by the facility's children. Conversations between Venny staff and the children revealed emotional attachments to the old building beyond what they anticipated:

> The building was a very decrepit old bunker ... holes in the floor, often toilets did not work ... it was dark and quite a hard space to actually work in ... But, [the children] did not mind it ... [they] loved it ... they were very attached to that old building. (Venny staff member)

Even though the old building had all these spatial and performance issues, it was a place that made these children feel at home, safe. For them, the idea of demolishing the building meant losing the place that provided a sense of belonging, security and adventure. The children expressed the stress of reconstruction:

> *I can't believe you're going to knock this down! I know it's not home but it could be home, it's got everything you need.* (Child cited in von der Borch 2011, 29)

Continuing in the old building under these conditions was not feasible, yet the reconstruction could have been devastating for the children. Instead, the design process was used to sensitively address the transition and to co-create new potential with the children. The design process involved the following enabling activities: spending time to understand, leveraging on existing relationships, co-creating and linking decision-making with larger social-ecological systems. These are elaborated in the following section.

Enabling Activities

Spending Time to Understand
The Venny has a long history of supporting at-risk children. Time to listen and to observe the stories of the place and the dynamics of the occupation before jumping into design solutions was essential to the process and outcome. According to the Venny's Manager and staff member, the architect spent a significant amount of time observing the dynamics of the place before creating the design brief and how it could support the programme. This time allowed the architect to form a deeper understanding of the significance of the place from a social perspective and also the risks associated with a 'brand new' design.

Irrespective of the physical qualities of a new building and how much 'spatial expertise' or knowledge (e.g. 'green' technologies) a practitioner brings, the time invested in being part of the place is critical. The time to understand the dynamics of the place is not replaceable by remote processes such as precedent studies. This time revealed insights about key intangibles that needed to be supported and enhanced, resulting in a project that sensitively approached the specific needs of the Venny community. This enabling activity, 'spending time to understand', has implications for contemporary practice in which the demands of quick and 'efficient' solutions are increasing. Without investing time, there are risks in missing opportunities or creating 'solutions' that often dismiss the intangibles (such as history, community agency, community wellbeing, citizenship) of a place.

Leveraging Existing Relationships
The process of leveraging existing relationships in this project worked on multiple levels. Within CoM, the project team promoted the Venny to secure funding. Within the Venny, staff worked closely with children to secure their input and engagement. In both contexts, existing relationships were leveraged with 'aim and purpose'. The reconstruction project started out of the need for a better physical space; however, it developed into a process of celebrating the Venny as a place, and more than a space. Venny staff leveraged their knowledge and experience to integrate children and young people into the design process.

Co-Creating with Children
The enabling activity of co-creation is best explored through the floor art project. This was a community art project to bring the stories of the old Venny and represent it on the floor of the new facility. It involved over 100 children. Some of the aspects captured on the new floor included the 'patina of time' from the children's work on the walls, ceiling and doors of the old building. During initial consultations it became evident that parts of the old building had layers of meaning for the children, who expressed this emotional connection through their desire to keep everything:

> Can't we just take this wall? ... we have to take the door. (Children cited in von der Borch 2011, 29)

As a response, the art project enabled the capture of loved aspects of the old building: children celebrated the old Venny by writing stories, drawing, painting, taking photographs, making imprints and a physical model. These place-stories were embedded in the floor of the new Venny, in a coloured spiral. This co-creation provided the transition between the old and the new facility and addressed the emotional connection that children expressed through making, exploring and celebrating. This was possible as a result of a collaboration between diverse stakeholders.

This activity highlights the role of agency in which each stakeholder is working within their individual sphere of influence (Hes and du Plessis 2015). It provides insights on the ripple effect within the design process created through cultivation of relationships.

Linking Decision-Making with Larger Social-Ecological Systems

During the design process, decisions were linked to larger systems such as environmental resources, urban greening, local context and so forth. The project team did this through facilitating the development of relationships and synergies between different systems and stakeholders. Some examples of those synergies included:

1. The programme, the staff, the building and the playground are linked to supporting children's development and potential, 'to develop life skills and resilience' (Our Community Pty Ltd 2014).
2. The process of reconstruction included ceremonies and rituals as modes of engagement to address the emotional connection of children by providing a thread of continuity between both places.
3. The roof was used as a testing ground for extensive green roofs. This feature was integrated to other systems and elements within the facility such as water storage, passive heating and cooling and solar energy, which resulted in the Venny building being water and energy positive.
4. The Venny is promoting ways of living within the ecological budget and in connection with other species through exploration, caring, creative engagement and education. For example, staff run gardening sessions, connecting children with processes of caring and growing, while acquiring skills that may be vital in their future. The playground includes animals such as hens and ducks running freely.

6.3.2 Case Study 2: El Guadual Early Childhood Development Center, Villa Rica, Cauca, Colombia

Background

El Guadual is the pilot project of a larger programme, 'early childhood comprehensive care strategy', dedicated to providing integral care for children between 0 and 5 years (Colombian Government 2013). Both the strategy and the pilot project were developed during a key transitional time in the socio-political context of Colombia. During the last six years, the country has been under negotiations of a contested reconciliation process between the national government and 'las FARC' Guerrilla, aiming to end the armed conflict that has affected the country since the 1960s. The armed conflict has affected the civilian population through horrible acts of violence including forced displacement, kidnapping, murder, violence against women and forced recruitment of children (Rodriguez and Sanchez 2012; Franco et al. 2006). The 'early childhood comprehensive care strategy' aimed to address this conflict by focusing on nurturing the potential of the youngest generations, through integration of services and actions to provide comprehensive care for children under 6 years old.

The strategy started in areas most impacted by the armed conflict and with a high percentage of children living in poverty. The aims of the project and the strategy are connected to larger purposes: the project is embedded in the early childhood strategy, and the strategy is interconnected to larger global development goals. The strategy aims to integrate services provided by a range of institutions, by supporting and encouraging collaboration between them. The intention is to make vital services for children (birth registration, vaccination, nutrition, health checks) easily accessible to families from low socio-economic populations by integrating all services in one place. The strategy identified a deficit in physical infrastructure and the need to create 1500 new early childhood centres across the country to provide adequate care to children in vulnerable conditions. This case study is the pilot project of these centres.

The Design Process
El Guadual was the result of a three-year participatory design and building process; the process has been considered as an exemplar precedent that fostered collaboration between a range of stakeholders including communities, public and private sectors and non-government organisations (BIAU 2014). The project emerged from multiple directions. The first was bottom-up, driven by the women from the local community known as 'communitarian mothers', who provide home-based childcare subsidised by the National Institute of Family Welfare (ICBF) (Bernal and Fernández 2013). The communitarian mothers approached the local mayor:

> The project was born out of the need to have a space for the children ... we, the communitarian mothers, offered our homes for them but these were very small spaces ... we had adapted them with a lot of love, but they were very small ... we, the communitarian mothers, invited the mayor and told him that we wanted a space for the children. He said ok, we will knock doors and he went to the presidency.... (Community Leader)

The second direction was the central government's own project team that was developing a participatory approach for the delivery of infrastructure (Architect I, Quinones and Economist S. Pineda, personal communication, January 15, 2014). The 'knocking the door' action that was started by the local women had a ripple effect which created the opportunity for this project to be the pilot in this location. The third direction was at the national level, with the design process for early childhood infrastructure considered to be a medium to support communities affected by the armed conflict and a way to start improving lives in those areas:

> Terror regimes have been institutionalised in many areas of the country making social service work life threatening. The First Lady and the Presidential Counsellor for Early Childhood understood the need to show that institutions were coming back to these regions, but wanted to do it in a way that would be impactful. By offering these communities the possibility to be part of the process, it became local and personal, not only political. Design processes were the avenue to create the desire for the institutions to return. (Architect D. Fedelman cited in Impact Design Hub 2015)

The project was enabled by 'timely convergence of willingness' and by individuals working within their own 'spheres of influence' (Hes and du Plessis 2015). Some stakeholders had a larger sphere of influence, such as the First Lady. However, without the actions of the local women and the local mayor the project would not have happened in the way that it did. The design process was a 'mediator' between diverse stakeholders to connect the creation of the infrastructure with other associated benefits such as new local jobs, training and community programmes, with an overarching aim focused on children's potential and development. Expanding capabilities of the design process beyond spatial outcomes were identified early by diverse stakeholders and resulted in an intergenerational participatory process.

Enabling Activities

Spending Time to Understand
Before exploring solutions, the project team needed to facilitate community participation and to develop an initial understanding of the local culture and environmental conditions. These initial stages included several visits to the area, design team members staying in the local houses, unstructured open dialogues with community members, mapping existing conditions of the home-based childcare houses and so forth. A design methodology to guide the process was created.

Searching and Acknowledging the Knowledge and Skills Gap

'Transdisciplinary design dialogues' (Wahl and Baxter 2008) were traced in the interviews from social, design, economic and governance perspectives. That is, the team recognised and sought additional skills, capabilities and knowledge. For example, the project included partnerships with a non-government organisation (NGO) that had been working for years in the region and had a good track of engagement and delivery of educational projects. The participatory workshops were facilitated by practitioners from disciplines such as social workers and psychologists, but the design team observed and participated in the consultations. The project was interconnected and interdependent to a national strategy with input from economists, sociologists, psychologists, policy makers, teachers and designers. The methodology developed through the project had ripples on the national strategy and vice versa.

Another example of acknowledging skills and knowledge gaps was the use of *guadua* (local bamboo), which was identified by the community as a preferred material. The design team did not have expertise in the material but were able to find practitioners who did. The material became a central feature of the design and the story of the project.

Inclusive and Intergenerational Participation

The NGO that guided the community participation programme invited people to dream about the centre through focus groups with children between 5- to 9-year-old, teenagers, community mothers, neighbours and families and local government representatives. The main users of the facility are children between 0 to 5 years old, considered too young to be involved in the participatory programme. Therefore, children between 5 to 9 years old participated and were prompted by the notion of leaving a positive legacy for their younger siblings. Some of the outcomes of this participatory process were:

1. Sense of ownership, stewardship and belonging
2. Uncovering and addressing conflict and potential displacement
3. Translating 'unachievable desires and expectations' into creative potential

The key to participation is for it to be real and not decorative participation, … and that comes from listening to the voices and proposals that the children have, that the community has, etc. it requires that architects are really willing to try to understand the community, to study it, and to somehow enable that the technical aspects meet the dreams of the people. (NGO leader)

Linking Decision-Making with Larger Social-Ecological Systems
Similar to the Venny, this project sits within a larger network of flows and systems. Project initiatives and decisions created interconnected benefits. For example, while the project was designed and built, the communitarian mothers were trained in early childhood education. The centre provides long-term employment with better salaries and working conditions compared with their previous experience. During the construction, local builders were trained and certified in construction methods. The strategy boosted collaboration between different sectors and created a more holistic and integrated approach to early childhood development and care for children in vulnerable conditions. The ripples from the design process extended to the creation of more than 30 other centres in different parts of the country, mainly funded by the government, that applied similar processes, while creating unique outcomes that responded to each location and community.

6.4 Defining the 'Benefit Driven Design Process' (BDDP)

These two case studies illustrate how the 'spatial' outcomes of design created an impact on the social-ecological systems in which they were placed. The consequences of design may be either positive or negative or both, influencing and influenced by ecological, social, cultural, psychological, political and economic dimensions of life (Awan et al. 2011). Similarly, the processes to create those outcomes can be used to generate beneficial or detrimental impacts on the larger systems. In other words, 'impact' is embedded in design processes, whether or not it is explicitly desired and acknowledged.

The case studies' enabling activities that lead to benefits beyond the spatial outcomes were:

- From the Venny: spending time to understand, leveraging existing relationships, co-creating and linking decision-making with larger social-ecological systems.

- From 'el Guadual': spending time to understand, searching and acknowledging the knowledge and skills gaps, inclusive and intergenerational participation, and linking decision-making with larger social-ecological systems

Based on the identification and analysis of these enabling activities, this research proposes the 'Benefit Driven Design Process' (BDDP), a set of design process capabilities that could support similar outcomes. The words 'benefit driven' are used to reflect the underlying positive psychology concept 'benefit mindset' which underpins this approach to design (Buchanan and Kern 2017).

The evolving approach of the BDDP argues that design processes with a sustained focus on benefit can create positive impacts to support the social-ecological system (Berkes and Folke 1998). Building on the idea that each individual has a sphere of influence (Hes and du Plessis 2015), within BDDP, every project, no matter its size, has a sphere of influence able to contribute both locally and to the larger social-ecological system in which it is embedded. The sphere of influence can vary from project to project as it is dependent on the particular contextual circumstances of the project. Design processes for urban interventions (including buildings) are understood as nodes where the different flows of a system interact (Ryan 2013; CLEAR 2016). For example, a school brings together the flows of students, parents, teachers, neighbours, learning pedagogies, materials, natural resources and built environment practitioners. All these flows converge in the creation of that school. These flows are also connected to larger social-ecological systems including social, natural, cultural, political and psychological dimensions. Therefore within the design process lies the potential to contribute to system flows, by creating the conditions to stimulate beneficial connections (Benne and Mang 2014; Hes and du Plessis 2015). BDDP is understood as a 'mediator' (Petrescu 2005) focusing on creating 'desired' and emerging benefits to the interconnected systems that converge during the process.

The BDDP aims to expand project outcomes through a series of interconnected enabling capabilities and processes. It is through the support of these enabling activities that the benefit of the project will emerge (Table 6.1).

These interrelated capabilities are connected with the enabling activities that were identified in the two case studies. These were then used to inform the design process for a project in Nepal.

Table 6.1 Benefit-driven design process: Enabling capabilities and activities

Benefit Driven Design Process

Enabling capabilities	Enabling activities	Purpose
Cultivating and nurturing relationships	Spending time to understand place	Generating benefits on the larger social-ecological systems (SES)
Stimulating active and inclusive participation	Leveraging on existing relationships	
Embracing transdisciplinary collaboration	Co-creating with the community	
	Linking decision making with larger social-ecological systems	
Activating individual and collective agency	Searching and acknowledging the knowledge and skills gaps	
Focusing on the creation of interconnected benefits	Enabling inclusive and intergenerational participation	

6.5 Applying BDDP in Nepal: Designing the *Purano Jhangajholi* Education Centre of Excellence

6.5.1 Background

The design process for a new school provided an opportunity to test the BDDP. This design research focused on identifying what could be achieved through using enabling activities to create the capabilities in the design and to affect the local social-ecological system. Central to this was the creation of mutual-beneficial partnerships (Mang and Reed 2012; CLEAR 2016) between pro bono design services and research and to generate feedback loops between discourse and action (Charlesworth 2014; Schneider and Till 2009). The design research project began when a non-for-profit organisation FONA, with operations in Nepal and Australia, approached the University of Melbourne. The project is located in Purano Jhangajholi, a village in rural south-eastern Nepal that was significantly affected by the 2015 earthquakes. The earthquake was the catalyst for the creation of FONA which envisioned this project as the opportunity to create place-based solutions by partnering with the local communities and international research and expertise (FONA 2017).

The design process applied different modes of engagement and collaboration with the local community (Figs. 6.1, 6.2, 6.3 and 6.4). It culminated in the development of a place-making strategic plan for the school. Construction of phase 1 is planned to start soon.

6.5.2 Enabling Capabilities in the School Design Process

Cultivating and nurturing relationships through spending time understanding the needs and aspirations of the local community. The process facilitated co-creation through engagement activities that included children, parents, community members and teachers. It also involved celebrations to reunite the community after the earthquake. Instrumental to this capability was the process of leveraging existing relationships. Connections with the community were built on the family relationships held by FONA's cofounders. The project team utilised their industry and academic network for in-kind contributions from disciplines of design, ecology, positive psychology and education.

Fig. 6.1 Visual representation of the new school. Source: incluDesign

Fig. 6.2 Visual representation showing the children of village in their future school. Source: incluDesign

Embracing transdisciplinary collaboration through workshops, frequent dialogues and close collaboration between the different stakeholders. A regenerative design workshop aimed to create integrated systems initiatives that responded to community and ecosystems needs and potential. The workshop led to longer-term collaborations and shaped key educational initiatives.

Stimulating active and inclusive participation through enabling co-creation with the community, by providing the atmosphere(s) to bring different voices to decision-making. Small, more intimate arrangements were provided to enable equal gender participation. Opportunities were created to hear the voices of every child that attended the school. Children provided drawings and written responses representing what they love about their village and their dreams for their new school. Participation taught the project team about cultural and spiritual assets, such as the spiritual significance of a tree located on site, which became central to the design and the story of the project.

Fig. 6.3 Children of the village looking for representations of themselves in their future school. Source: FONA

Activating individual and collective agency through co-creation of narratives that can inspire transformation inwards and outwards (Mang and Haggard 2016). The process co-created narratives focusing on a future of possibilities for the village after the earthquake. These narratives are based on regenerative principles of building capacity and enabling new potential (Mang and Reed 2012). The process inspired actions from local and international collaborators towards making the project and its interrelated initiatives happen. The story of a local engineer who initially wanted to cut down all the trees to make space for the buildings illustrates this process of activating agency. Through his involvement in this process, he has instead become a local advocate towards development that can co-exist with the environmental and cultural heritage (FONA 2017).

Fig. 6.4 Cultural ceremony and performance celebrating a new beginning. Source: FONA

Focusing on the creation of interconnected benefits through working towards the creation of mutually beneficial relationships, by connecting design-related interventions with larger social-ecological systems. Some of the interconnected benefits that the process enabled are:

1. Training for local teachers
2. Reciprocal learning experiences between the local village and international volunteers
3. Initial steps towards the co-creation of a new educational model with the community that supports deep connections from being (connecting with self), relating (connecting to others) and doing (through co-creation). The model aims to celebrate local wisdom, to embrace and improve local agricultural practices and to enable intergenerational learning and new local business.

6.6 Conclusions

This chapter has presented two case studies that illustrated how design outcomes can transcend the provision of physical infrastructure, resulting in much greater benefits. From these case studies the enabling activities were identified that gave the design process the capability to influence these outcomes. These processes were then tested in the design of a new school in Nepal.

The Benefit Driven Design Process that can support the development of an eco-city, connecting its physical and social infrastructure to its ecosystems, is:

- Cultivating and nurturing relationship between all stakeholders including local communities and the nonhuman
- Stimulating active and inclusive participation through spending the time with the stakeholders to co-create the outcome
- Embracing transdisciplinary collaboration through valuing all skills and creating the atmospheres to build upon diverse aspirations
- Activating individual and collective agency through connecting all stakeholders to the central narrative of the outcome
- Focusing on the creation of interconnected benefits through creating mutually beneficial relationships and partnerships.

6.7 Take-Home Tool: Enabling Activities in the Benefit Driven Design Process

The enabling activities are part of an iterative process. These activities do not follow a particular order and can be adapted to the particular circumstances of each project:

- Spending time to understand place
- Leveraging on existing relationships
- Co-creating with the community
- Linking decision-making with larger social-ecological systems
- Searching and acknowledging the knowledge and skills gaps
- Enabling inclusive and intergenerational participation

References

Allpress, Brent, Robyn Barnacle, Lesley Duxbury, and Elizabeth Grierson. 2012. *Supervising Practices for Postgraduate Research in Art, Architecture and Design*, Educational Futures: Rethinking Theory and Practice. Vol. 57. Rotterdam: Sense Publishers.

Awan, Nishat, Tatjana Schneider, and Jeremy Till. 2011. *Spatial Agency: Other Ways of Doing Architecture*. New York: Routledge.

Benne, Beatrice, and Pamela Mang. 2014. Working Regeneratively Across Scales - Insights from Nature Applied to the Built Environment. *Journal of Cleaner Production* 109: 42–52.

Berkes, Fikret, and Carl Folke. 1998. *Linking Social and Ecological Systems: Management Practices and Social Mechanisms for Building Resilience*. Cambridge: Cambridge University Press.

Bernal, Raquel, and Camila Fernández. 2013. Subsidized Childcare and Child Development in Colombia: Effects of Hogares Comunitarios de Bienestar as a Function of Timing and Length of Exposure. *Social Science & Medicine* 97: 241–249.

BIAU. 2014. Archivo de La Bienal Iberoamericana de Arquitectura Y Urbanismo [Archive of the Ibero-American Architecture and Urbanism Biennale]. *IX -BIAU*. http://www.bienalesdearquitectura.es.

Buchanan, Ash, and Margaret Kern. 2017. The Benefit Mindset: The Psychology of Contribution and Everyday Leadership. *International Journal of Wellbeing* 7 (1): 1–11.

Charlesworth, Esther. 2014. *Humanitarian Architecture: 15 Stories of Architects Working After Disaster*. London and New York: Routledge.

CLEAR. 2016. Lenses Facilitator Manual: How to Create Living Environments in Natural, Social and Economic Systems [Manual]. http://clearabundance.org.

Colombian Government. 2013. *Early Childhood Comprehensive Care Strategy: Political, Technical and Management Fundamentals "de Cero a Siempre."*

Downton, Peter. 2013. *Design Research Revised*. Melbourne: Elizabeth James Productions.

FONA. 2017. FONA Big Ideas Practical Solutions. Accessed March 8, 2017. https://www.fona.org.au.

Franco, Saúl, Clara Mercedes Suarez, Claudia Beatriz Naranjo, Liliana Carolina Báez, and Patricia Rozo. 2006. The Effects of the Armed Conflict on the Life and Health in Colombia. *Ciência & Saúde Coletiva* 11 (2): 349–361.

Gill, Tim. 2007. *No Fear: Growing up in a Risk Averse Society*. London: Calouste Gulbenkian Foundation.

Hes, Dominique, and Chrisna du Plessis. 2015. *Designing for Hope*. New York: Routledge.

Impact Design Hub. 2015. The Reality of Building a Social Impact Design Project. https://impactdesignhub.org.

Mang, Pamela, and Ben Haggard. 2016. *Regenerative Development and Design: A Framework for Evolving Sustainability*. New York: John Wiley Sons Inc.

Mang, Pamela, and Bill Reed. 2012. Designing from Place: A Regenerative Framework and Methodology. *Building Research & Information* 40 (1): 23–38.

Moustakas, Clark E. 1990. *Heuristic Research: Design, Methodology, and Applications*. London: SAGE Publications.

Our Community Pty Ltd. 2014. The Venny. http://www.melbourne.vic.gov.au/aboutmelbourne/projectsandinitiatives/majorprojects/pages/thevenny.aspx.

Petrescu, Doina. 2005. Losing Control, Keeping Desire. In *Architecture and Participation*, ed. Peter Blundell-Jones, Doina Petrescu, and Jeremy Till, 43–64. London: Taylor & Francis.

Rodriguez, Catherine, and Fabio Sanchez. 2012. Armed Conflict Exposure, Human Capital Investments, and Child Labor: Evidence from Colombia. *Defence and Peace Economics* 23 (2): 161–184.

Ryan, Chris. 2013. Eco-Acupuncture: Designing and Facilitating Pathways for Urban Transformation, for a Resilient Low-Carbon Future. *Journal of Cleaner Production* 50 (July): 189–199.

Schneider, Tatjana, and Jeremy Till. 2009. Beyond Discourse: Notes on Spatial Agency. *Footprint: Delft Architecture Theory Journal* 4: 97–111.

Stockholm Resilience Center. 2014. What Is Resilience? An Introduction to Social-Ecological Research. http://www.stockholmresilience.org.

von der Borch, Danielle. 2011. *Memory Needs a Place to Rest*. Melbourne Institute for Experimental and Creative Art Therapy.

Wahl, D.C., and Seaton Baxter. 2008. The Designer's Role in Facilitating Sustainable Solutions. *MIT Press Design Issues* 24 (2): 72–83.

Yin, Robert K. 2014. *Case Study Research: Design and Methods*. Los Angeles: SAGE.

CHAPTER 7

The Problem, the Potential, the Future: Creating a Thriving Future

Dominique Hes and Judy Bush

Abstract This chapter summarises the key lessons and tools presented by the chapters of the book, and discusses how we need to shift from identifying the *problem* to recognising the *potential* in our identification and resolutions of the eco-city. Using the scenario of the restoration of an urban waterway and its ecosystem services, the chapter explores how each tool and approach can help to contribute to the transition to thriving eco-cities.

Keywords Thriving • Urban ecosystems • Governance • Community participation

7.1 INTRODUCTION

This chapter summarises the key lessons and tools presented by the chapters of the book and discusses how we need to shift from problem to potential in our identification and resolutions of the eco-city. The chapter explores how each tool and approach can help contribute to overcoming problems by reframing them as potentials and developing solutions.

D. Hes (✉) • J. Bush
Thrive Research Hub, Faculty of Architecture, Building and Planning,
The University of Melbourne, Parkville, VIC, Australia

© The Author(s) 2018
D. Hes, J. Bush (eds.), *Enabling Eco-Cities*,
https://doi.org/10.1007/978-981-10-7320-5_7

We review the '10 steps to understanding the potential of place', presented in Chap. 2, and in doing so, weave in the take-home tools from Chaps. 3, 4, 5, and 6 to show how together these elaborate the transition to eco-cities. Following this, we test how these can be expressed and operationalised through considering examples of restoring urban ecosystem services. We apply these in a thought exercise using a real scenario that has been occurring here in Melbourne for the last 30 years, the restoration of Merri Creek. In doing so, our intention is to go beyond the conceptual understanding of how these tools could be applied and uncover what the tangible outcomes could be.

7.2 Shifting from Identifying *Problems* to Creating *Potential*

We need to shift from a focus on solving problems to creating potential in the development and adaptation of our cities. An example of understanding the shift from problem to potential and of 'future making' in action is the example of bullying in schools. We all know that no school has ever really 'solved' a bullying problem. But what many schools are doing today to address this challenge is co-creating futures building on the potential of their schools.

Instead of focusing on their problems, the school's community comes together to ask—what brings our school fully alive? What are the seeds of potential that exist within those who are acting as bullies, that want to be expressed? How can they contribute to the seeds of potential within the broader school community? This co-creation activity has been shown to elevate schools to new levels of potential and vitality—and issues like bullying fall away as part of the process (Buchanan 2017).

While simple problems may be solvable, problems in complex systems are unlikely to be 'solved' or even solvable (Meadows 2008). Instead, we advocate shifting the focus from diagnosing the *problem*, towards understanding, fostering and nourishing the *potential* within the complex systems of thriving eco-cities. In doing so, this opens space and opportunities for creativity and innovation (Box 1).

> **Box 1 City of Melbourne's strategic planning for urban ecology**
> City of Melbourne's award-winning *Urban Forest Strategy* incorporated innovative approaches and creative responses to the problem of managing tree canopy in a growing, densifying, changing city (CoM 2012). The Strategy identified the issues and challenges of an ageing
>
> *(contiuned)*

> (contiuned)
> tree population, limited water and soil moisture, climate change, urban heat island and extreme heat, and population increase and urban intensification. Solutions focused on measures to increase canopy cover, soil moisture and water quality. While the Urban Forest Strategy inspired the identification of a number of the policy success factors highlighted in Chap. 4, including the importance of community engagement, it largely focuses on proposing solutions to *problems*, rather than the *potential* of ecology to create urban ecosystems. City of Melbourne's more recent urban nature strategy, *Nature in the city: Thriving biodiversity and healthy ecosystems* (CoM 2017) arguably represents a shift towards a more 'regenerative' approach, with its focus on identifying goals, rather than issues and their associated solutions.

7.3 Bringing the *Thriving Eco-City* Tools Together

This book has introduced a series of tools that can support any developer, government or city maker to be able to influence the generation of an eco-city.

The ten steps outlined in Chap. 2 establish a framework through which to guide the entire process. The tools and approaches presented in Chaps. 3, 4, 5, and 6 help to fill out these steps with specific actions that can be undertaken. These are elaborated in this section and then applied to the Merri Creek's restoration scenario in the following section.

1. Create a core team of people who participate in the process from development of the understanding of place to the identification and implementation of the priorities.

    This core team is the foundation for the ability of a project to retain its intentions and aspirations throughout implementation. These are the holders of the narrative of the project's potential, the group of people that continually looks back at opportunities and asks the question whether these opportunities provide the context for the project and its stakeholders to thrive. Though placed here in step one, this core team will emerge from the process of the project. What is critical for this core team is that they are not just outwardly looking at the project but also inwardly reflecting on who they are and their role within the project. This is critical because this reflection stops projects stagnating, as it provides opportunities for continual development, growth and new energy. The core team provides the focal point from which to build engagement and participation in the project's creation and design (Chaps. 3 and 6) and to foster the project's 'champions' (Chap. 4).

2. Map the physical stocks and flows of the place such as hydrological, geomorphological and ecological that bring a place to life.

   Step two is around capturing the biophysical data of the place. It creates an understanding, a foundation from which to design and plan those activities that will underpin the eco-city journey. This is largely a data mining exercise looking at soils, ecosystems, water cycles, climate, resources, energy and all those physical flows that will affect an actual site. Collecting and looking at this data will start to surface patterns; these patterns are like the personality of the place. We relate this to a person as a way of illustrating the power of understanding the pattern from the data. If you have a good friend or partner and you see them hunched over, grey and reserved when usually they are effervescence and vibrant you can tell that there is an issue. You do not need to test their blood pressure, understand if their iron is low or carry out psychoanalysis before you ask them what's wrong; you know this person and you can see that they're not their usual self, and by observing this change in pattern you can then investigate further. You also, for the most part, know how to help them. Mapping the stocks and flows, spending time to understand place, is a key 'enabling activity' (Chap. 6).

3. Map the non-physical aspects that bring a place to life—its history, culture, methods of exchange and so on.

   Beyond the physical stocks and flows that affect the place, there are the non-physical flows of knowledge, creativity, community, exchange and value (more than just what is often represented by money), spirituality and so forth. Adding and mapping a sense of what these are for a place will bring to the surface interesting patterns that often mirror those seen in the physical stocks and flows. Bringing together steps two and three allows a response to place that comes from what is actually present. Developing the ability to collect this kind of data and then to identify the patterns will increase the ability to create opportunities aligned with how things already work 'here'. Paula Underwood Spencer (quoted in Mang et al. 2016, 209–210) illustrates the power of observing pattern, as integral to how indigenous peoples build and embed understandings of the complexity of the world (Underwood Spencer 1990):

> As a part of the Native American training I received from my father, one of the aspects of perception that I was asked to understand was the distinction between Hawk and Eagle, between the way Hawk perceives and the way Eagle perceives. In the shamanic tradition, you gain that appreciation by what is considered to be direct experience. However, the distinction—once learned—is easily translated into Western logical sequential language structure.
> When hunting, Hawk sees Mouse ... and dives directly for it.
> When hunting, Eagle sees the whole pattern ... sees movement in the general pattern ... and dives for the movement, learning only later that it is a mouse.
> What we are talking about here is Specificity and Wholeness.

The non-physical aspects, the multiple creative perspectives (Chap. 3), narratives (Chap. 4) and niches underpin the place-based system complexity (Chap. 5) and the necessity for investing time towards mapping and understanding these place aspects (Chap. 6).

4. Using these flows, look through major events over the place's history and look at the flows that had an impact.

Once the physical and the non-physical data has been collected, one of the ways to surface patterns is to look through the history of that place and to map those stocks and flows across time. So, for example, during the Second World War when there was food shortage, the introduced rabbit population was decimated across the Victorian landscape. This saw the return of a lot of native vegetation. There is therefore a negative relationship between the introduced rabbits and native vegetation, and one of the ways to increase native vegetation is to reduce the number of rabbits. Now this is a simple example which we Australians intuitively know, but it shows how those things, that might be important for a site, can be informed by looking through history. These can also be understood as experiments, the successes and failures of which provide insight to the system (Chap. 5), reinforcing the importance of monitoring, evaluation and reflection (Chap. 4).

5. Using this understanding, look at the relationships between the flows and the place that created these impacts.

    This process will allow the start of connecting the relationships between the stocks and flows both physical and non-physical and the place. For example, if we go back to a person: my daughter loves to draw, paint and be creative. Now I could want her to be a tennis player. I could spend a lot of money on lessons and a lot of energy arguing, threatening and ultimately bribing her to go to lessons, and she will probably learn to be a decent tennis player. Instead, I could support her creativity by working with her natural inclinations, her capabilities and her essence, never needing to waste energy 'forcing her to do it', leaving us both with the joy and energy of creating and thriving together.

    Similarly, as we start observing the patterns of the place we start developing the ability to see its essence. This does require time: if my daughter was a stranger I would not know how to channel her essence. But once you have this understanding, it allows for meaningful and effective design of initiatives that will support a place to reach its potential, move to creating the opportunities for thriving and create meaningful connection to place: 'a sense of place offers a unifying story of belonging that weaves together our world and inspires us to re-imagine not only how we live and lead—but the nature of the world itself' (Jones 2014, 1).

    One of the roles of the core team will then be to hold on to the stories, the patterns, the data that have led to the understanding of the essence of place so that all decisions can be referenced back to this. The relationships between the flows and the place, as well as between the project's participants, enable alliances and partnerships (Chap. 4) and leveraging existing relationships (Chap. 6).

6. Identify key patterns of this place and develop a sense of the role this place plays in the larger system.

    This process will not only lead to an understanding of the place itself but also its relationship to the places around it, to this larger system. At this point the team working on the development of this place will start looking at how it is influenced by and influences the systems around it. This is critical, again, because an eco-city aims to create thriving for the whole, and each place as part of that whole is not about just creating benefit for a component of the city but creating benefit for the whole. This complexity can be understood in three levels (Mang et al. 2016, 56): the project, the proximate whole and its greater whole, together representing nested systems. This is really about looking at the ripples the project will have for its neighbourhood and beyond.

An understanding of place can be built up by applying the take-home tools: the engagement created by creative practice (Chap. 3), building coherent narratives from multiplicity (Chap. 4), embracing system complexity (Chap. 5), the Benefit Driven Design Process' enablers and linking with the larger social-ecological system (Chap. 6).

7. Use 'Smart: S3' to identify unique opportunities for development based on the positive relationships mapped above.

Once stocks and flows and their relationships are understood and you have a sense of the essence of the place, it then becomes more straightforward to start identifying opportunities for increasing the vitality and viability of those stocks, flows and relationships. Unique opportunities that can support the potential of place, for example my daughter's creativity, begin to emerge. The Benefit Driven Design Process enables the identification and design of these (Chap. 6). This is the concept design phase, the dreaming of opportunities and the creation of ideas. This is where the trajectory towards eco-cities (Chap. 4) helps in developing ideas on how to support this transition. Understanding the existing stocks and flows and their relationships can then lead to identifying the types of measures that will be most effective in shifting the system and building the eco-city.

8. Use 'Specialisation: S3' to focus on the unique patterns and strengths of the place by initiating a critical mass of activity and capabilities that builds on the identified positive relationships.

In this step the concept of niches (Chap. 5) and small-scale experimentation (Chap. 3) are used to identify and undertake activities which start to explore the effectiveness of the opportunities developed in earlier steps. In the shifts towards an ecological worldview and looking towards nature to inform innovation, the intention is to start small and recognise the effectiveness of interventions, as being critical to achieving the potential of a place. This is critical as systems are so complex that sometimes unintended consequences arise, either positive or negative, that cannot be foreseen—experimentation allows these to be understood.

9. Use 'Strategy: S3' to identify a limited set of priorities for development and where to concentrate investment. These priorities should be co-created with the people of the place.

   This step builds from knowledge of place, and its larger context within nested systems, as well as the process of creative experimentation. The process of identifying a limited set of priorities can often mean an inherently competitive selection process between options. This can result in only pursuing those ideas that are perceived to provide the greatest value and trading-off benefits. However, regenerative development offers an alternative approach that tries to avoid trade-offs, by engaging with and valuing different, even seemingly opposing ideas (Hes and du Plessis 2015, Mang et al. 2016). It harnesses creativity to develop new ideas that reconcile and integrate the best aspects of the variety of approaches. In doing so, it can potentially 'increase the value or benefit for all levels of the system … [by] harmonizing, aligning or attuning' (Hes and du Plessis 2015, 124).

   This approach asks project teams to look at the greater potential that competing options may align on. This is where it is critical to look for *potential* and not *problem resolution* discussed earlier. Aligning potential needs to be a co-creative process, a process that benefits from interdisciplinary input and the ability to experiment, play, reflect and create. The ways to do this are through co-creation (Chaps. 3 and 6) and through experimentation and implementation testing in niches (Chap. 5). Implementation of the arising priorities and actions will be supported by people when they have participated in the co-creation, have ownership of the decisions and understand the narrative (Chap. 4).

10. Integrate a feedback and reflection process both for the development of the viability, vitality and ability to thrive of the place as well as those involved in the project.

    Having an effective feedback loop and reflection process is critical to any project throughout its conception and implementation. The conception stage involves reflection around alignment with the core principles and values of the project and reflection for each person participating, on their ability to support the process to achieve its highest potential outcomes. In the implementation stage, there needs to be a process for collecting results of progress, an effective reflection and adaptation process to again ensure the outcomes are aligning the core ideas. Within the implementation process, the internal reflection continues to be critical as well. Projects can be derailed by a key decision maker or person with particularly strong personality traits; regenerative development is as much about developing the capacity of those involved as it is about developing the project outcomes.

Furthermore, for the value, experience and learning to be captured from experimentation and new approaches, feedback and reflection (Chap. 4) to identify and celebrate the successes as well as failures (Chap. 5) is essential to underpin ongoing implementation and creativity. Without this, it risks stagnating into business-as-usual replication rather than continued creative development.

7.4 Applying the *Thriving Eco-City* Tools: Merri Creek's Restoration

Merri Creek flows from the foothills of the Great Dividing Range south to Port Phillip Bay in south-east Australia. It flows through the lands of the Wurundjeri Willam, the traditional owners and custodians of the region. Over the last 200 years, a major city has developed on its banks and across its catchment—Melbourne. Merri Creek, like other urban waterways and green spaces, has suffered the effects of urbanisation: increased impervious surfaces creating sudden floods; water pollution, litter and rubbish dumping, often particularly visible after floods; vegetation has been cleared and creek banks reshaped. There have also been larger threats: proposed construction of a freeway, overhead powerlines and other infrastructure. Urban waterways have been seen as corridors of otherwise vacant land that can accommodate such structures. However, in the face of these threats, local residents, communities and local governments came together to restore and revitalise the creek.

In the last 30 years, many sections of Merri Creek have been transformed from weedy unloved littered wastelands to landscapes of native plants to which the native fauna, birds, reptiles, insects and frogs are returning, and which are cherished by Melbournians. Merri Creek's restoration has created spaces for and valued by its human and non-human residents and visitors; its restoration is based on both ecology and people (who are part of its ecology). Merri Creek demonstrates that urban environmental sustainability and restoration is possible and achievable but that activism and action is often necessary. As such, Merri Creek's restoration provides a case study to explore the application of the thriving eco-city tools.

1. Create a core team of people who participate in the process from development of the understanding of place to the identification and implementation of the priorities

2. Map aspects of the place such as hydrological, geomorphological, ecological and so on

Team: In response to threats to Merri Creek from proposals for freeway construction and engineered responses to flooding that involved channelising and concreting the creek, smaller groups of residents and individual local governments coalesced to form larger alliances: Merri Creek Management Committee and Friends of Merri Creek. Both groups celebrated 25 years of existence in 2014. They continued to be involved over the 25 years holding the vision for a thriving abundant Merri Creek

Biophysical context: The landscape of the Port Phillip region is a result of the combination of climate, soils, topography and Aboriginal custodianship and land management. Today's urban landscape is a result of these continuing biophysical and cultural factors and processes, overlaid by European colonisation and settlement and subsequent urban planning, design and development and land and water management. Notwithstanding these processes and disruptions to the region's ecosystems, Melbourne is a city 'rich in biodiversity', though careful urban planning and management is required to maintain and enhance biodiversity values (Ives et al. 2013)

To underpin and inform Merri Creek's restoration, detailed research was undertaken to document the hydrology, flora, fauna, geology, cultural heritage and recreational uses (MCMC 2009)

Merri Creek includes wetlands and waterways, escarpments and native grasslands. It provides habitat to a wide range of animals, small and large, and for plants, including rare and threatened species (MCMC 2009). It is also the location for urban infrastructure, including the city's storm water system

3. Map the stocks and flows that bring a place to life—its history, natural flows, climate, money and so on

Cultural context, stocks and flows: The region had already been occupied for at least 40,000 years; it is within the traditional lands of the Aboriginal people of the Wurundjeri and Boonwerung tribes, of the Kulin nation (Presland 2008; Flannery 2002). The Aboriginal connection with the land is a deep and powerful, bidirectional relationship in which the landscape shaped the people and the people shaped the landscape (CoM and MSI 2016). 'In looking at the natural history of an area, we are also looking at aspects of local Aboriginal culture' (Presland 2008, 203). Aboriginal connections with land, embodied within the land stewardship concept of 'caring for Country', emphasise the fundamental connections between environment, society and economy, 'there is no economy without environment, no environment without society, no society without economy and so on' (CoM and MSI 2016, 12) Today, the creek and its banks and parklands provide vital and valuable spaces for people, urban dwellers, many of whom may have few other opportunities for contact with nature, green space and non-human biodiversity. It includes both wild and manicured spaces, a shared walking and cycling trail, picnic areas, a market garden and community gardens and secluded spaces for quiet and contemplation. Merri Creek is the muse for artists, novelists and poets

4. Using these flows, look through major events over the place's history, and look at the flows that had an impact—positive and negative	***History:*** Urbanisation of the creek's catchment and banks created a polluted, unloved corridor. Neighbouring houses turned their backs to the creek; the creek banks were lined with back fences and littered with dumped rubbish and pollution. During heavy rains, the creek and surrounding areas flooded, prompting calls for flood control measures. After particularly severe flooding in 1974, engineered solutions to flood mitigation were proposed that would have involved straightening, channelising and concrete lining the creek and, with proposals for freeway construction and extension of overhead electricity powerlines, would have completed its destructive transformation into an open drain (PIRG 1975). This is an example of a single linear attempt to solve a problem based on the flow of water, rather than looking at the potential of the other flows to create a natural thriving place where the water flow becomes a life giving force not a problem
5. Using this understanding, look at the relationships between the flows and the place that created these impacts	***Relationship between history, stocks and flows:*** Instead of trying to remove floodwater as quickly as possible from urban areas, understandings of catchment processes led to the creation of flood basins, wetlands and a whole-of-catchment approach. In this way, Merri Creek avoided the fate of concrete channelisation; wetland habitat and its associated insects, frogs and birds started returning to the creek Using the research on Merri Creek's biophysical and cultural heritage context, the growing familiarity of the creek environs by the members of the core team, and with the input of artists and writers, a *six-season calendar* was developed. The calendar reflected Aboriginal understandings of seasons and the rhythms and cycles of this place, rather than a transported and transposed understanding of seasons originally applied to the region by its British colonisers. The six-season calendar celebrated the theatre of late summer thunderstorms across the dry landscape and the wattle blossoms of early spring, reflected the growing intimate knowledge of and connection with the place
6. Identify key patterns of this place and develop a sense of the role this place plays in the larger system—this will help identify its story	***Larger context, nested systems:*** Merri Creek is a tributary of the Yarra River. It is part of the larger biophysical system of the Yarra River catchment and the Port Phillip region surrounding the bay. As such, the creek creates a habitat linkage between the foothills of the Great Dividing Range, the Yarra River catchment and the Port Philip region When Melbourne was established by British colonists on the banks of the Yarra River, the Port Philip region was a 'temperate Kakadu', the abundance of its wetlands creating 'a most beautiful and bountiful region … billabongs and swamps were sprinkled right around the bay, and they teemed with brolgas, magpie-geese, Cape Barren geese, swans, ducks, eels and frogs' (Flannery 2002, 7–8). The region settled by British colonists in 1835 had already shaped and been shaped by Aboriginal people's stewardship and economy for tens of thousands of years

(*continued*)

(contiuned)

7. Use 'Smart: S3' to identify unique opportunities for development based on the positive relationships mapped above	***Audit—place and team skills:*** In the last 30 years, many sections of Merri Creek have been transformed from weedy unloved wastelands to landscapes of native plants to which the native fauna, birds, reptiles, insects and frogs are returning and which are cherished by Melbournians. Merri Creek demonstrates that urban environmental sustainability and restoration is possible and achievable, but that activism and action is often necessary
8. Use 'Specialisation: S3' to focus on the unique patterns and strengths of the place by initiating a critical mass of activity and capabilities that builds on the identified positive relationships	***Experiments and opportunities:*** Merri Creek's local communities have resisted such threats and are actively working to replant and restore habitats, reinstating ecological burning regimes for native grasslands and providing opportunities for community involvement in the processes, including with school activities and citizen science In addition to regular community planting days (Bush et al. 2003), festivals, artworks and celebrations have strengthened people's connection to Merri Creek. These have included the *Return of the Kingfisher festival*, which celebrated habitat and biodiversity, the *Multicultural and Refugee Planting* festival that created opportunities for putting down roots—both literal (plant-based) and figurative (new residents and new communities) and a travelling photography exhibition, that traversed the libraries across the Merri Creek catchment, celebrating 25 years of community efforts for habitat restoration and reinforcing a sense of connection across the broader catchment
9. Use 'Strategy: S3' to identify a limited set of priorities for development where to concentrate investment. These priorities should be co-created with the people of the place	***Priorities:*** As cities grow and develop, pressure increases on unbuilt land, even from those who love its open spaces. The competition for space, function and purpose for Merri Creek includes contests over habitat for native animals and birds versus dog walking, bicycles versus walkers on the shared paths and sporting grounds versus native grasslands on the flat plains beside the creek. The reconciling force is the creek itself! It creates a narrative that flows across land, across land uses, between mountains and sea, connecting and creating opportunity. The Merri Creek strategy, which defines the priorities for the creek, has been co-created by the core team using its relationships with and input from local communities, local governments, water and power utilities and catchment organisations
10. Integrate a feedback and reflection process both for the development of the viability, viability and ability to thrive of the place as well as those involved in the project.	***Feedback, reflection:*** This step is particularly important for projects such as Merri Creek's restoration is to continue to foster creativity and a willingness to experiment and trial new approaches and to welcome new participants to the core team, throughout its 30 years of implementation. This requires a balance between maintaining its core narrative and vision, while also being open to new ideas, new approaches, new knowledge and changing priorities This step also reinforces the ongoing co-creation of the project and reflects the inherent interwoven and non-linear, non-sequential character of the *10 steps to a thriving eco-city*

The Merri Creek case study offers a narrative developed over a period of 30 years, telling of the importance of the green and blue spaces that the creek provides. The elements highlighted in this chapter perhaps paint an overly positive picture. The story of its restoration also contains conflict, experimental failures and disappointments and ongoing sites of destruction and thoughtless disregard or disrespect for its life-supporting values. We would contend that using a more *potential*-driven process could minimise the problems caused by those who do not understand the role of the creek and its contributions.

A more detailed exploration of the creek's restoration and of the story of its stocks, flows and relationships would more fully explore and reveal these aspects as well. However, through a mixture of creative practice, community passion and willingness to invest in the protection and restoration of the creek, many of the urban development impacts are being addressed. People see the potential of the creek and are working towards supporting and enhancing that potential.

7.5 Conclusions

If the future of cities is a hub of thriving, abundance, innovation and the driving of human civilisation into the future, and we acknowledge the critical importance of our coexistence and evolution with nature, then we will need to transition our cities to eco-cities. If this is driven by the concepts presented at the start of this book, those of the ecological worldview, then this transition will require ways to engage differently in our city making. In this book, we have attempted to do this by presenting our research in regenerative development and its application through smart specialisation. We have discussed how as part of this transition we can shift from action and activism of a few towards all becoming environmental citizens, shifting the conversation from passive consumption to active participation through Benefit Driven Design Processes and the opportunities of engagement and celebration through creative practices. We have looked at how to apply the outcomes of these engagements to place through experimentation in niches. And finally, how to embed these in policy to ensure their effective uptake.

We hope that through our attempts to highlight the practical aspects of our research, we have provided the opportunity for readers to see how this work fits within their own roles of transitioning towards an eco-city. We hope that our contributions add to fostering stronger relationships with urban stocks and flows, and to empowering the ongoing co-creation of thriving eco-cities.

References

Buchanan, Ash. 2017. We Can't Problem Solve our Way to a Thriving Future. *Medium.com*. https://medium.com/benefit-mindset/problem-solving-future-making-9561596bf5b4. Accessed October 6, 2017.

Bush, Judy, Barb Miles, and Brian Bainbridge. 2003. Merri Creek: Managing an Urban Waterway for People and Nature. *Ecological Management and Restoration* 4 (3): 170–179.

CoM. 2012. *Urban Forest Strategy. Making a Great City Greener. 2012–2032*. Melbourne: City of Melbourne.

———. 2017. *Nature in the City. Thriving Biodiversity and Healthy Ecosystems*. Melbourne: City of Melbourne.

CoM and MSI. 2016. *Caring for Country: An Urban Application. The Possibilities for Melbourne*. Melbourne: City of Melbourne and Monash Sustainability Institute.

Flannery, Tim. 2002. *The Birth of Melbourne*. Melbourne: Text Publishing.

Hes, Dominique, and Chrisna du Plessis. 2015. *Designing for Hope: Pathways to Regenerative Sustainability*. Abingdon: Routledge.

Ives, Christopher D., Ruth Beilin, Ascelin Gordon, Dave Kendal, Amy K. Hahs, and Mark J. McDonnell. 2013. Local Assessment of Melbourne: The Biodiversity and Social-Ecological Dynamics of Melbourne, Australia. In *Urbanization, Biodiversity and Ecosystem Services: Challenges and Opportunities. A Global Assessment*, ed. Thomas Elmqvist, Michail Fragkias, Julie Goodness, Burak Güneralp, Peter J. Marcotullio, Robert I. McDonald, Susan Parnell, Maria Schewenius, Marte Sendstad, Karen C. Seto, and Cathy Wilkinson, 385–407. Dordrecht: Springer.

Jones, Michael. 2014. *The Soul of Place: Re-Imagining Leadership Through Nature, Art and Community*. Toronto: Friesen Press.

Mang, Pamela, Ben Haggard, and Regenesis. 2016. *Regenerative Development and Design: A Framework for Evolving Sustainability*. Hoboken, NJ: Wiley.

MCMC. 2009. *Merri Creek and Environs Strategy 2009–2014*. Brunswick East: Merri Creek Management Committee.

Meadows, Donella. 2008. *Thinking in Systems: A Primer*. London: Earthscan.

PIRG. 1975. *The Merri Creek Study: A Review of Urban Creek Management, Past, Present, Future*. Melbourne: Public Interest Research Group.

Presland, Gary. 2008. *The Place for a Village: How Nature Has Shaped the City of Melbourne*. Melbourne: Museum Victoria Publishing.

Underwood Spencer, Paula. 1990. A Native American Worldview. *Noetic Sciences Review*.

Index

A
Action, activism, 2, 22, 23, 31, 34, 35, 38, 49, 52, 56, 58, 66, 69, 71, 74, 90, 91, 96, 97, 101, 104, 110, 111, 116, 117, 120, 121
Adaptation, 10, 30, 47, 48, 74, 110, 116
Adaptive, 14, 70, 71, 74, 75, 77, 78, 80, 82, 90
Altruism, 37
Anthropocentric, 22
Architect, architecture, ix, 2, 5, 80, 93, 96, 98
Arts
  artists, 23, 26, 27, 34, 79, 80, 118, 119
  community arts, 6, 35–37, 94
  participatory arts, 34–37

B
Beauty, 30, 31, 37
Behaviour change, 24
Biodiversity, 2, 4–6, 29, 30, 44–46, 49, 50, 52, 57, 111, 118, 120

Biophysical, 3, 4, 6, 10, 11, 45, 112, 118, 119

C
Case study
  Armidale, Australia, 24
  Black Gully Festival, Australia, 26–27
  The Bower Stage, Australia, 24, 35–38
  Cheonggyecheon, Seoul, S. Korea, 11
  El Guadal, Colombia, 95–99
  Emscher River, Germany, 18
  Ephemera Festival, 26–27
  EU S3 Platform, 15
  European Regional Development Fund, 16
  FONA, 101
  Melbourne, Australia, ix, 92–95
  Merri Creek, Australia, 121
  Purano Jhangajholi, Nepal, 101–105
  Ruhr Valley, Germany, 16
  The Venny, Australia, 92–95

© The Author(s) 2018
D. Hes, J. Bush (Eds.), *Enabling Eco-Cities*,
https://doi.org/10.1007/978-981-10-7320-5

Case study (*cont.*)
  Vancouver, BC, Canada, 79, 80
  Zollverein UNESCO World
    Heritage Site, Germany, 17
Change, processes of change
  dynamic cycle, 77
  incremental, 78
  s-curve, 77, 78
  systemic, 75
  trajectory, 71
  transition, 5, 10
Children, 30–36, 38, 92–99, 102–104
  child care, 35, 95–97, 99
Civil society, 16
Climate change, 3, 4, 6, 31, 47–51, 66, 69, 77, 90, 111
Collaboration, 19, 26, 27, 29, 35, 36, 66, 79, 80, 94, 96, 99, 102, 103, 106
Collective, collectivity, 23–26, 31, 34, 37, 90, 104, 106
Communication, 4, 6, 23, 35–37, 57, 58, 92, 93, 96, 99
Communitarian mothers, 96, 99
Community arts, 6, 35–37, 94
Complexity, 14, 24, 54, 69, 82, 90, 113–115
  complex systems, 57, 110
Conflict, 23, 58, 69, 95–98, 121
Connection, ix, x, 4, 6, 23, 24, 31, 33, 35, 37, 44, 94, 95, 100, 102, 105, 114, 118–120
Creativity, x, 2, 5, 7, 22–38, 110, 112, 114–117, 120

D
Design process, 6, 29, 30, 90–106, 121

E
Eco-drama, 32
Ecofeminism, 22
Ecological ethics, 25
Ecological worldview, 3, 4, 115, 121
Economy, 10, 14, 15, 71, 118, 119
Ecoscenography, 6, 25–27
Ecosystems
  ecosystem services, 44–46, 49, 56, 57
  urban ecosystems, 11, 46, 48–50, 110
Eco-theatre, 26
Emotion, 24, 26, 37, 92, 94, 95
Empathy, 23, 24, 26, 35, 37
Empowerment, 6, 16, 23–25, 35, 38, 121
Enabler, 90, 115
Enabling process, 6, 33, 90–106, 112
Energy, water and resources, ix, 2, 4, 37
Engagement, ix, 4–6, 15, 19, 22, 25, 27, 36, 37, 48, 53–56, 58, 91, 92, 94, 95, 98, 102, 111, 112, 115, 121
Entrepreneur, 5, 10
  institutional entrepreneur, 16, 18
Entrepreneurial Discovery Process (EDP), 15, 16
Environmental citizenship, stewardship, 24, 37, 44, 55, 98, 118, 119
Equity, 35, 36
Evaluation, 16, 48, 52, 59, 113
Experiment, experimental, 11, 14, 59, 68, 82, 113, 116, 120, 121

F
Families, 12, 30–33, 96, 98, 102
Functionality
  mono-functionality, 6, 44, 45, 56, 59
  multi-functionality, 6, 44, 57, 70

G

Gardening, 25, 27, 95
Geography, 73, 76
Governance
  inclusive, 15
  multi-level, 15
  participatory, 15
  role of governance, 49

H

Health and well-being, 2
Hope, 23, 26, 37, 121

I

Incentives, 53–56, 69, 72, 80
Industry, industrial, 17, 18, 80
Influence, sphere of influence, 11, 38, 56, 59, 72, 73, 79, 80, 94, 97, 100, 106, 111, 114
Innovation, ix, x, 5, 6, 10, 11, 14–16, 22–38, 53–58, 66–82, 110, 115, 121
Institutional, 16, 18, 71
Interdisciplinary, 75, 116

J

Justice, vii

L

Learning, 15, 16, 23, 24, 48, 59, 76, 82, 91, 100, 105, 113, 117
Low carbon cities, 4

M

Materialism, 37
Mechanistic worldview, 3, 4
Mediators, 90, 97, 100
Mixed methods research, 27
Monitoring, 15, 16, 48, 52, 59, 113
Multidisciplinary, 70
Multi-Level Perspective (MLP), 47, 68, 71–75, 78–80
Multi-phase concept, 71
Multisensory, 24
Municipality, municipal, local government, 18, 48, 51, 66, 69, 92, 98, 117, 118, 120

N

Narrative, x, 3–6, 24, 25, 35, 37, 38, 44, 45, 54, 58, 104, 106, 111, 113, 115, 116, 120, 121
Nature, 2, 4, 5, 10, 12, 22, 25, 32, 37, 44, 46, 47, 72, 90, 111, 114, 115, 118, 121
Nature-based solutions, 44, 46, 47
Niche, x, 6, 10, 11, 14, 16, 47, 66–82, 113, 115, 116, 121

P

Panarchy, 74, 77–79
Participation, participatory design, 6, 14, 15, 18, 19, 24–26, 33, 53, 91, 96, 98–100, 103, 106, 112, 121
Place
  essence of, 5, 10, 15, 114, 115
  placed-based, 22, 78, 90, 99, 111
  place-making, 102
  story of, 5, 12, 79
  uniqueness of, 14
Plants, 11, 25–27, 29–31, 46, 117, 118, 120

Policy
  policy domains, 44, 48–50, 54, 57, 60
  policy instruments, mechanisms, 51–56
Positive contribution, x, 22, 91
Private sector, 16, 96

Q
Quadruple Helix, 16

R
Regenerative development, ix, 2, 4, 5, 10–19, 23, 116, 117, 121
Regime, 47, 67, 68, 72, 75, 78–80, 97, 120
Relationships, 2–5, 10–12, 14, 19, 25, 93–95, 99, 102, 105, 106, 113–115, 118–121
Resilience, ix, 2, 6, 23, 35, 37, 66–68, 70, 71, 73–82, 91, 95
Revitalisation, 16
Risk, 15, 37, 57, 82, 92, 93, 117

S
Scale, x, 3, 6, 44, 46, 56, 66–82, 90, 115
Smart specialisation, 5, 10, 15, 16, 121
  S3 strategy, 15, 16, 19, 115, 120
Social capital, 34, 37
Social-ecological systems (SES), 4, 5, 7, 37, 45, 54, 59, 66, 69–71, 74–78, 90, 93, 95, 99–101, 105, 106, 115
Social learning, 16
Socio-technical, 2, 11, 45, 54, 71, 72, 74–78
Stage design, 6, 25, 27
Stakeholders, 5, 10, 15, 19, 58, 80, 94–97, 103, 106, 111

Story, 4, 6, 10, 11, 14, 19, 24, 25, 27, 30, 32, 36, 37, 45, 80, 93, 94, 98, 103, 104, 114, 119, 121
  story telling, 24–27, 32, 33
Structuration theory, 72
Sustainability discourse, 22
Sustainability transitions, ix, 5, 6, 10–16, 47, 66–68, 71–79, 81, 82
Systems
  feedback loops, 101, 116
  stocks, flows and relationships, 5, 115, 121

T
Technical, 70, 74, 78–80, 99
Technological, 4, 16, 71, 72, 76
Theatre, 6, 24, 26, 31, 119
  immersive theatre, 24–26
Thriving, ix, x, 2–7, 10, 11, 22, 34, 36, 44, 90–106, 109–121
Tourist, tourism, 17, 18
Transdisciplinary, 22, 23, 90–106
Transition management (TM), 47, 48, 68, 75

U
Urban and regional development, 16
Urban ecology, 45, 110
Urban green space, 6, 44–49, 51, 53–60
  urban green roofs and walls, 53, 57
Urban heat, 6, 12, 14, 111
  urban heat island, 12, 14, 111
Urban nature, 37, 111
Urban planning, 6, 45, 49, 66–69, 71, 73–82, 118
Urban policies, 6, 47, 57, 59, 60, 76
Urban renewal, 14
Urban waterway, 7, 117

V
Vegetal crafting, 30
Vision, 2, 4, 7, 44, 45, 48, 52, 54, 55, 58, 59, 118, 120

W
Waste, 2, 50, 66, 114
 zero waste, 33
Worldview, 3–7, 22, 71

Printed by Printforce, the Netherlands